Praise for Adderall Blues

"Blues is a compelling firsthand account ... Robinson wrote *Adderall Blues* not only to share his personal story but to inspire others to progressively reimagine the way they support those with ADHD."

— **Daniel Patterson,** *Huffington Post*

"I loved the power in the writer's voice as well as how genuine the read was. I found the perspective of the character to be as I was hearing a story from a friend and helping him along his journey. *Adderall Blues* by Brian J. Robinson is defiantly an educational and inspiring read as it focuses on the strengths rather than the flaws that come with every person. Mental illness or not, power is within all of us. The descriptions of the feelings and emotion can be felt through each page and with every word."

— **Chelsea Girard, Book Reviewer at Bibliobeautybooks**

"The tone is accessible and inviting, instantly pulling the reader in to the world of the young boy with vivid descriptions and a pacing that mirrors what is going on in his mind. It's a great read for anyone—whether they have ADHD, or are looking to understand it better. Beyond the topic, it's also simply just a good book, with both funny and touching personal stories that are easy to relate to."

— **Madina Papadopoulos, Author of** *The Step-Spinsters*

"Few books on this subject have explored the positive side of ADHD and this alone makes *Adderall Blues* an important read."

— **Indie Book Reviews**

"Finally! A blunt but objective book that debunks ADHD labels and exposes the unfortunate and limiting ways in which societal norms inhibit brilliance. Mr. Robinson's journey of interrupted genius is a first and important step toward a much-needed societal shift in which learning disabilities are celebrated . . . not diagnosed"

 — **Dr. Peter J. McDonald, PhD. (Educational Policy)**

"A wonderful, in-your-face book relating one young person's struggles with Attention Deficit Disorder . . ."

 — **Dr. Ned Hallowell M.D., Harvard Medicine and Author of *Driven to Distraction***

"Brian Robinson poignantly exposes the flaws in our current educational philosophy and challenges us to rethink ADHD as a cure for slowed innovation rather than an illness in need of taming."

 — **Damian Brenes Dominguez, Founder Spil Creative, Inc.**

"Brian has captured, without exception, the frustration and incite into the world of attention deficit disorder. His stories are relatable. I commend his writing skills and purpose.

 — **Dr. Samuel Schenker, MD (Neurologist)**

"*Adderall Blues* tells an engaging tale of a young man finding his way in the world while learning about himself and his ADHD. Robinson's story is an important lesson in understanding how to unlock the potential of young people, especially those diagnosed with attention deficit disorders."

 — **A. Corcoran (Former Educator, Master of Public Policy)**

"The chronicals of Brian's life events are so captivating and intense that I couldn't put the book down. Eye opening and an emotional roller coaster. This story will encourage more people with ADHD, who likely have similar feelings about Adderall, to share their story to raise awareness of the issues Brian posits."

— **Nicole Stokes, Published Research Scientist, Regeneron Pharmaceuticals**

"A much needed memoir to highlight a crucial topic in today's society. Mr. Robinson's story is witty, engaging, humorous and thought-provoking; a bold confession that brings to the forefront a struggle that so many people deal with on a daily basis. This is a must read for anyone who's life may have been touched by ADHD or other learning disabilities. "

— **Dr. Rama Ayyala, MD, Columbia University Medical Center**

"This refreshingly honest account of living with ADHD reframes both the struggles and gifts that come along with this stigmatized diagnosis. A passionate reminder of the need for our education system to nurture the unique mind of each student and warns us about the far-reaching dangers of forcing conformity in the classroom."

— **Pamela Mendelsohn, LMSW**

Adderall Blues
by Brian J. Robinson

ISBN 978-1-63393-433-7

Published by

 köehlerbooks ™

210 60th Street
Virginia Beach, VA 23451
800-435-4811
www.koehlerbooks.com

Adderall Blues

By Brian J. Robinson

Table of Contents

Chapter 1
Dead End

It occurred to me, like a spontaneous lightning bolt of neuro-stimulative ambition, that it was time to write my book. I know what you are thinking. I have absolutely no business writing a book, especially something autobiographical in nature. Stories about one's self are reserved for sports heroes, influential historical figures, and celebrities. I fit none of the above categories.

I am a Jewish twenty-three-year-old from an upper-middle-class, suburban family who fell into the world of finance. Quite typical, you might say. White-collar bred and white-collar destined. And sure, I would even agree with you, except for one thing: Absolutely nothing about the twenty-three years inside this head of mine has been the least bit ordinary. I have come to realize that my experiences and my perspective on the world are representative of what a childhood ADHD diagnosis might very well explain.

Though I never put much thought into that branding until now.

I always knew that I had a tendency to see things differently from others, or as some refer to them, "the Neurotypicals." My earliest memory is a lucid visual of my father smiling with love in his eyes as he picked me up out of my crib. I was crying and must have been age two at the time. Looking back, I knew, even then, that if there was one person I would be able to count on in this world, one person who would love and stand by me no matter what, it would be my father. If not for the careful consideration and undying faith that both he and, to an equal degree, my mother have shown me throughout the years, especially when I was a young child, the outcome of my life after that could very well be drastically different.

We lived in Toms River, New Jersey, home of the 1998 Little League World Series Champions, from 1985 to 1990. Apparently, my crying pleas for freedom from the barred cage that was my crib transformed into violent statements of protest where I would shake the entire structure until it fell over. Later, I would just climb out, as it seemed a bit more sensible.

If nothing else, Toms River taught me to be physically tough at an early age. The kids in and around Foothill Court were rough. Besides Timmy Williamson, I was the youngest on the cul-de-sac, roughhousing and playing kickball until the sun came down. Brian Williamson was my best friend at the time and his kid brother, Timmy, would march behind us wherever Brian and I went.

It is truly amazing to me how the universe really is tied together by the most delicate and transparent of forces, like ever-shifting layers of indistinguishable energy. Most people do not think twice about the power and magnitude of the energy that encompasses our existence. Our introduction to these matters is taught in school, or so I am told. Looking back, I realize I never heard a word that was said to me there. From kindergarten through college, most of what was addressed to me in the form of spoken language was as foreign as the Mandarin I would encounter in Shanghai.

It is like watching a big-screen HD TV with the most technologically progressive picture clarity money can buy. This imaginary TV magnifies perceptions of the big picture to even further degrees of intensity, all the while reducing the sound quality to mere vibrations. Luckily, when I am in tune, these sound vibrations synthesize themselves into visual images. Sound must be converted to pictures for me to process, in my own way, what someone is saying. It is like having a screen in my mind's eye.

Welcome to my custom IMAX theatre, where the shiny buttered popcorn and Junior Mints are plentiful and Albert Einstein and the rest of the spatially inclined autistics enjoy VIP seating and always share a good laugh. Of course, we get a younger following as well, especially around report card time, where a D average in school is rewarded with a free Coke and a daytime matinee on the house. It is the least that can be done after a full marking period of trying to fit ourselves into an educational system designed for the masses, or in mathematical terms, the distribution of individuals closest to the mean. Is it really any wonder why mathematical and scientific leadership is deteriorating in this country? Some of the most brilliant scientific thinkers, the visual thinkers whose thought processes are innately universal and capable of a different type of creative abstraction, the type of thinking that is necessary for scientific innovation, are falling through the cracks of the educational system, having never been given a shot to explore their expansive minds. Albert Einstein, who is also known to think in pictures, was at one point a high-school dropout who struggled enormously with his education.

Einstein thought, when stuck in a dead-end job later in his life, that maybe he should work some physics problems in his spare time. Some of the imaginative thinkers of our time are the visual thinkers, and often, as I suspect from my own intimate personal experience with the issue, certain types of learning potential are often muted by learning problems. I am sure Einstein would agree that learning aptitude is linked to the educational environment. If am thinking conceptually, in pictures, and my teacher is subjecting me to tedious rote memorization in words, then I might as well be sitting in a classroom pondering my own thoughts and marching to the beat of my own drum in Shanghai, China. There must be something to be said for a culture, whose written language is pictographic, that is leaving the United States in the dust as the global scientific leaders and innovators of modern civilization. Riddle me that.

The fact is, our country is lagging behind in the highly competitive landscape of scientific innovation and technological progression. With the decline of manufacturing and our dismal status as scientific pioneers on a global scale, clearly something must change. It is demoralizing that we are in such poor shape intellectually, despite the obvious fact that we still remain a wealthy economic superpower. Complacency and a lack of intellectual and scientific progress hinder any country fighting to maintain economic supremacy.

The right educational system and the active pursuit of knowledge and innovation is the DNA of a truly great society. We cannot afford to let some of the brightest minds in our country struggle through life as unrealized potential simply because we are so enslaved by our repetitive methods of thought and policy and methodology. Individuals, who could, with the proper teaching style and encouragement, contribute a great deal to society end up living life believing they are failures, or worse. The most brilliant and unique minds also tend to be the most fragile. Given rigid societal standards and the cookie-cutter idea of intelligence and high performance, it is no wonder that some of our greatest gifts walk the streets and are a fertile, untapped natural resource.

The public educational system must will itself toward innovation if we are to compete with the intellectual powerhouses of the East. Just as preventive medicine aims to address and deal with a health problem before it is actually a problem, so too must we transform in a time of relative stability before this problem becomes much more urgent. It is painful to watch the political process constantly react to dilemmas and crises only when situations become near desperate. Chaotic times are the breeding grounds for rushed and poorly thought-out decisions. I fear that one day soon we will wake up and realize that it is too late to act effectively. Potential continued economic supremacy in a global economy is inextricably linked to a long-term commitment to maximizing the intellectual capital of this country. Change must be implemented before our road to opportunity becomes a dead end.

Okay, now I'll get off my soapbox and tell you a story.

Chapter 2
Bri Bri Land

I really thought I was dumb for a long time. It's just that I process information in an unorthodox manner. Just so you have an idea, my world exists as a lucid display of interconnected concepts that make up the whole. These concepts are abstractions; I see ideas and they manifest visually as derivative lines of thought. I get lost in a hypnotic stream of images. I'll look at dirt and think country, from country I see space, from space, notions of identity and culture, and from culture I see change, or time. Suddenly I am pondering distance. All the while, as my tangent carries on, I often won't see what's around me externally, or I'll see both.

It's like I am living in two worlds at once, and I need to manage them in order to stay functional, but they can never intersect. It's quite entertaining. Even when I am physically there, I am far away. I can literally have a telephone conversation with someone and go through the motions of human interaction while simultaneously I am carried off into a seemingly altogether different universe. There is no real way to control my thoughts. They are like wind blowing, taking on different forms with a disregard for stillness. Amusingly, I've walked into more trees than I'd like to admit while thinking—or, more accurately, dreaming awake. I just shrug it off with a smile and keep on trucking.

So, they say I have Attention Deficit Hyperactivity Disorder, or ADHD. Admittedly, I'm not a great listener. Sometimes, all I hear is sound with no meaning when somebody talks to me. If I am not visualizing what is being said, I am not thinking at all. Or more succinctly put, I am rocketing into what one of my best friends in high school cleverly described as "Bri Bri Land." Now don't get me wrong; once I dock into the ether I am in a world that is undeniably my own. Bri Bri Land, as I see it, is where the magic of abstraction and intuitive universal knowledge combine with enough energy for one hell of a quantum leap into the great depths of my semi-conscious mind. It's a surreal mechanism that I'm used to. It's very much a gift and a curse. And it is only recently, amidst the worst transformational struggle I have ever been through, that I finally realized the truth about this state of mind—*I wasn't hearing what people were saying.*

I didn't know that was abnormal or even that I wasn't processing. I just wasn't self-aware enough to perceive that anything was different between me and others—until I was twenty-three. It is only now that I realize that when someone is talking to me, without some sort of external intervention or an immense effort toward concentration, which often fails, I'll be elsewhere in a matter of seconds.

Let's back up though, because this state of mind has been the source of so much joy, so much misery, and so much endless amusement to others that I must do the best I can to tell this story from the bottom up.

* * *

My full name is Brian Jeffrey Robinson. My father is Neil Robinson and my mother is the lovely Ellen Robinson—Mrs. Robinson, as so many have happily pointed out. I also have a younger sister, Jill. She is a fair-skinned blonde with big blue eyes and a pretty face. I have seen her only intermittently throughout my life ever since she was sent to a boarding school for children with special needs when she was about twelve.

Second grade was the golden age of my academic achievement. I was enrolled in Ranney School, a snobby private school where I had to put on an itchy suit and tie every day and where I used to dominate the tire swing. I took pride in giving my classmates the ride of their life on that swing, a ride that took them out of the real world for a while and into my own playful universe. My favorite move was The Tornado; I would dedicate a good ten seconds to building a strong rotational momentum and right before the release I would nudge the chain I had been holding onto against the very momentum that I worked so hard to create. The nudge created a sweet spinning torque, the result being an entire swing revolving in one direction, while rotating the exact opposite direction. I used to like to think that my tire swing extravaganza was the closest I could get to creating the sensation of being inside the vacuum of a tornado. Any ride that can completely disorient your sense of direction is worth the price of admission. I never rode the tornado myself. A couple of my schoolyard chums used to try to duplicate it for me but never came close. Somehow, that was okay, though. My mind was its own tornado.

It was always a mystery to me that second grade was the only time I managed to get straight As. I used to outperform on tests the kids who eventually ended up going to Ivy League schools. Despite my aptitude, I would hand in writing assignments on notebook paper with a clear disregard for the margins. My handwriting was atrocious and I was literally writing all over the paper as if I was painting. To this day, I cannot write in between the lines of school notebook paper, spreadsheets, charts, and so forth. It is as if the lines or boxes in front of me do not exist. Thank goodness for word processing, because half the time I cannot read my own writing.

Third grade was a piece of cake as well. I loved my friends but I was extremely unchallenged academically. The best part about being in third grade was having our own lockers. Stephanie Jenkins and I would play a game where I would happily volunteer to tuck myself in her locker. She would close the door and we both thought it was the greatest thing. It was pitch black and I could barely move a muscle, but I wouldn't have preferred to be anywhere else. Looking back, I think I enjoyed it so much because it gave me the same sensation I felt in my childhood forts. I would spend hours building the most

elaborate blanket forts, which were air-tight with little green
army figures sometimes placed strategically outside to create an
even grander façade of fortification. This makes sense to me as
an adult.

While I have long outgrown my blanket fort days, the shield
that I have developed, or my shell, as one of my high school
girlfriends called it, protected me from the outside world. I
suppose I had it because I was afraid nobody would understand
me if they really got to know me. Interestingly, the girl who used
to shut me into darkness and giggle endlessly, proved to be the
very young woman who would send me on my path toward
liberation over a decade later.

Fifth grade started what I see as the beginning of the end.
Years and years of underachievement slowly chiseled away at
the foundation of what was once thought to be excellence. As a
child, I was often uncooperative, to say the least. Mischief and
exploration defined my somewhat chaotic self. Destruction was
the name of my game as a child and still managed to manifest
itself in other forms as I got older.

One day, while tracing the creek behind my house through
the untouched backwoods of the small suburban town where I
grew up, my best friend Jay and I stumbled upon an actual boat
stuck in the mud. The boat was laying there practically etched
into the sandy creek bottom and with specs of rot throughout
its underside. The creek it was laying in was by no means a
river, with only inches to work with at times. Perhaps there
a time where it ran deep and powerful like a river, only to be
downgraded by nature to a creek years later. Fifth grade was a
tough year for me, and things did not get easier for a while.

I began to realize soon that I was struck, just like that boat,
and even with the best parents one could ever have and regular
trips to the psychiatrist, no one could possibly understand,
including myself, why I'd get angry sometimes. Why wasn't I
doing well in school anymore? Why was I getting into trouble
all the time? I felt alone, and thought it was always going to
be that way, and despite possessing a mind that would just not
shut off, I was still human in every sense of the word. I was just
a kid trying to figure himself, and the world, out. I was also a
survivor. I didn't have a lot of friends around this time in my

life, but I wouldn't let myself be picked on, either. I got in a fair number of scuffles with some bigger kids back in the day, and they weren't any better for it. Survival is one our most base and animalistic imperatives, and the will to live and live in my own way is not something I ever seriously questioned. Despite my troubles my spirit, was always strong, though that strength has certainly been put to the test.

Chapter 3
Hebrew School

Here's the thing about time. I just don't get it!

I cannot come to terms with sequence because I cannot come to terms with the man-made nature of time. Time is a man-made invention, and my mind has trouble with artificial concepts. Time is simply the human intellect's attempt to quantify change, which is the only constant in the universe. Measuring time, as humans love to do, is our way of creating expectations of change. I would say we gave it a great shot. Whereas most people view life as a series of moments, my intuitive grasp is that there is only one moment: the same moment. The sun will rise and set and we can certainly call it a new day for the sake of creating a schedule for ourselves, the economy, etc. But from a truly logical standpoint, don't you think it's artificial? My days at Hebrew school certainly felt that way.

* * *

Hebrew school to me was the most insufferable, and dare I say traumatic, experience of my life. Like Chinese water torture, it just never ended. First Sunday school, and then Hebrew school twice a week. Just like in regular school, I never heard much of what the teacher was telling me, but that does not for a second mean that I didn't know exactly where they were coming from. They were clearly trying to brainwash me.

The people who ran the system had the audacity to try to inflict their belief system on *me*. Yes, I think it's important to be a good person, and religion tries to teach that by using metaphors, but these people seriously believed that all these stories from the Old Testament actually happened. Meanwhile, I was expected to show up and listen to what the holy one commanded us to do without any justification for his reasoning. He could tell a bear to go dye his hair magenta and make an origami statue out of honey wax paper, and true believers would absolutely obey. "Sure, Mr. God, sir. Whatever you say, Mr. God." While I am not opposed to the idea of faith or believing in something that is not provable or tested by science, imposing ideas against someone's will has a name—tyranny.

I still cannot bear to step in the wretched hell hole that is Temple Shalom. For years, the Hebrew school classroom brought out the worst in me. Having ADHD, six hours of regular school is enough, but to then go to this place to sit still and learn questionable facts for two hours after school twice a week was pure lunacy. The first hour consisted of general religious study—I think. I truly do not believe I heard or learned anything. I cannot recall how many times I was yelled at, had teachers call my house, or was suspended. I was accused of being disruptive and instigating others while they were being indoctrinated like I was Socrates corrupting the youth and refusing to believe in the gods of the city.

I do remember the one day that epitomizes the anger and rage I had for this institution. Mrs. B., whatever her name was, had just finished telling us the story of when Abraham, in accordance with God's wishes, carried his own son to the top of a mountain with every intent to slay him. God asked him to do this as a display of his undying loyalty to him. Immediately, I raised my hand and with more rage than I could even attempt to cover up—not that I'd want to—I spoke my mind and my heart. I told her with all due respect, if God, or anyone else for that matter, instructed me to take my own son up a mountain and slay him, I would tell him to go to hell. God sounded sadistic to me. As I said, I cannot even recall which number suspension that resulted in.

The second hour was just as unbearable as the first. No, it was worse, because it required active participation in learning a very difficult language that I would never use. Hebrew, while admittedly a historically important language, is like learning Latin. It's a useless language, unless you're inside a cathedral or in the state of Israel. If I were to ever go to Israel, I rationalized as a child, I was sure they would speak enough English for me to get by. But anyway, that class would put me into complete emotional disarray.

Learning Hebrew was symbolic of everything that was wrong with the world at that time. I wasn't paying attention, didn't want to be there, and the classroom smelled funny. I did my best to tune out, but inevitably I would get called on. Of course, I was not on the right page and even after the class informed me of the page number, I couldn't read Hebrew anyway. The teacher and I would go through the same ritual every class and waste each other's time in the process. I had decided the moment I arrived at Temple Shalom that I would not learn anything they taught me. This is in stark contrast to normal school, where I tried hard but was beginning to think by sophomore year in high school that I was not very smart anymore.

Imagine how maddening it would be if you could not respond intelligently at times when people spoke to you. Most of the time, I was just guessing which words had come out of another's mouth while doing my best to piece together a response based on context and body language. Every once in a while, though, the barrier would drop, and I could process spoken language beautifully and bounce answers back at people with charisma. I did best when moving—physically.

When I am walking, my ability to focus is drastically improved. I never really understood why I would get these temporary highs where I would feel stimulated and outwardly confident. In retrospect, I see that kinetics was always involved. But there was no telling when the next wave of outward charm and intelligence would come. They certainly did not come around too often at Temple Shalom, where requiring students to sit still seemed to be etched on stone tablets.

* * *

By twelve years old, they had enough of me. The happiest news I heard in a long time came when they told my parents they don't want me back. I hadn't wanted them for years and I was never given the option of telling them to take a hike. Hallelujah! I had been expelled! Joy to the world! No more Hebrew school. Maybe it was when I punted the Old Testament across the parking lot that did it. Or maybe it was when I took my shirt off and drew happy faces all over my body during a Hebrew lesson. Didn't know, didn't care. Mom and dad were pissed; I had to go to more psychiatrist appointments, and I really couldn't have cared less. Here's some advice: If you ever have an ADHD child who hates religious school, just let him skip it. Religion is the type of thing that if you want to seek out later in life, you can. But please don't shove it down your children's throats.

Looking back, though, it wasn't a total loss. There were two individuals that I did take a liking to. Rabbi Weiner struck me a as a man of great character. Imagine my surprise when, in one last desperate attempt to get me to become a bar mitzvah, I was introduced to my new Hebrew tutor, a wonderful woman who proved to be a very important person in my life. I knew instantly that she was different. When I meet an authority figure who I actually trust, I am more than respectful to them. My ability to size up character and integrity rarely fails me, and Mrs. C. passed my initial scan with flying colors. She sat me down and reasoned with me instead of shoving garbage down my throat. She told me her son was just like me when he was my age, and had the same issues.

I learned Hebrew and received my bar mitzvah, despite being expelled from the school, because Mrs. C. was on my side, and because it meant the world to my parents. But I still think it was a waste of time. I firmly believe that a non-religious person is just as capable of living a moral life as a religious person. I follow my own intuitive path rather than relying on what a book of any sort can tell me about being good or how to live. All humans have the capacity to be good; it is just a matter of choice. If religion makes you a better person, then study it. If you are killing people in the name of your own idea of what God should be, you ought to re-evaluate the foundational principles of your moral doctrine. I'm not here to declare whether no religion is better than having religion, though we all should be given a choice. Don't you think?

* * *

A lot of kids grow up hating religious school for many of the same reasons that I did. It's just harder when you have ADHD as a child. It's a very oppositional and defiant mindset to begin with. Combine that with poor impulse control and utter fatigue from regular—secular—scholastics, and you're in for an eruption. No amount of Ritalin or psychotherapy helped me to get through any of it. This is not to say that people with ADHD cannot, or do not want to, be religious. As with people in general, there are variations. I do think that a lot of kids with ADHD may end up having a bad experience with these types of institutions, though, and might be better off with self-study.

I can accurately pinpoint a real change in myself to when I was fourteen and no longer had to attend Hebrew school. The anger subsided, and I began to chill out with high school on the horizon. I had also convinced my parents to let me out of private school and into public school so I could have friends that were close by, and more importantly, I didn't have to wear that awful suit and tie, which was more like a noose around my neck. Suddenly, I was free every afternoon to hang out with my friends, or watch TV, or do anything I wanted. High school was the next phase in my life, and it gave me the freedom to work toward happiness.

Chapter 4
High School

It was one of the first days of freshman year at Holmdel High School in central suburban New Jersey. I sat down next to Rob Pepitone, a friend of mine, whose house was in the same neighborhood as Jay's. Rob was really smart. It was the type of thing you could recognize, even when you're fourteen and you are all pretty dumb.

With the Chinese water torture of Hebrew school behind me, the Jews were finally leaving me alone. I was less anxious and really just happy to be able to move on with my life. I was pulling mostly Bs and some As. I still had very little capacity to absorb much of what was being said in class, but I read all my reading assignments and did all my homework, which was enough to for me to understand the lessons and get by. For me, self-study was the key to academic success. Later, I learned that this is most certainly the case for the majority of those similarly afflicted.

Sophomore year was dismal for me academically. Most of my end-of-the-year Cs spent a great deal of time in D territory. The reasoning was simple enough; I wasn't going home and studying like I had been. I decided I was as smart as I needed to be and my time and energy were better spent biking across Route 35 and hanging out with my friends on the other side of town. I had also joined the wrestling team, which emphasized physical toughness over scholastic achievement. Academics were getting harder and

I didn't care. What relevance was there in mitochondria being the powerhouse of the eukaryotic cell? If x squared equals y cubed plus your mom divided by three, how fast is the train going when it reaches Guam? Who the hell cares?

By the end of sophomore year biology class I was so fed up with the enormous amount of effort I wasn't putting in to learn these things that I raised my hand and asked Mr. Schwartz, the biology teacher, what he would do if I pulled the emergency shower in the back of the science lab next to the eye wash station. He told me that as long I was standing right under it and mopped it up afterward, it wouldn't be a problem. Mr. Schwartz learned a lesson that day as I stood there in my navy-blue surfboard shorts and sopping wet white T-shirt, mop in hand. I would go the extra mile to amuse myself, or punish myself—whatever that was. I felt baptized by the nihilism of it.

Later that year, in Mr. Saneki's psychology class, I was handed a reminder that maybe I was a little bit smart, but not in the right ways. In the spirit of what is really philosophy instead of psychology, Mr. Saneki handed us all square pieces of paper and wrote in large font on the chalkboard: THERE IS NO ABSOLUTE TRUTH. Immediately, I felt a ferocious rush of stimulation. It actually felt like a fuzzy scattering just below my skull. He wanted each of us to write a short answer, anonymously, in response to this statement, and hand it in. Any random, guttural reaction would do. I do not think I have ever seen an entire class stupefy in front of my eyes as I did that day. Even the A students in the front of the classroom looked uncomfortable, as if to say, "We did not prepare for this. There was no mention of this in last night's preparatory notes." Looking back, it marks the only time I ever felt that stimulative effect in response to a lesson in high school.

I wrote impulsively and sloppily with my trusty left hand: IF THERE IS NO SUCH THING AS ABSOLUTE TRUTH, I MUST BE LOOKING AT THE ONLY ABSOLUTE TRUTH. Then I folded the paper and submitted it.

He went through every response out loud. Each response was lamer than the next. My insecurity about being a Jewish kid with what was perceived to be at most average academic abilities caused me to be angry with myself a lot of the time. For those of you not familiar with the Jewish tradition of academic excellence, the archetype of the good Jewish boy begins with a stellar academic record followed by admittance to an Ivy League school. There are certain sub-Ivys that are acceptable—Emory, Vanderbilt, Washington University . . . Beyond undergraduate studies, the greatest joy for a Jewish mother is for her son to go off to medical school and be a doctor. Short of that, law school will more than suffice—again, especially if we are talking Ivy League or top tier.

I believe that in recent years Asian-Americans have begun to beat the Jews at their own game, institutionalizing a whole new quantum of parental pressure and towering expectations. So, if there was a moment in a classroom where I actually felt smart, then I was going to bask in it—hell, even write about it years later.

When he read my answer, Mr. Saneki's jaw dropped as I saw him reread it just to make sure. He finally muttered, "It's too bad whoever wrote this didn't sign their name, because I would have given them extra credit."

I raised my hand immediately, but I doubt he believed it. He liked me because I was a wrestler, but I would have been among the last in the class he would have expected as the scribe of that answer. I don't think any of my teachers thought of me as especially bright. I was actually pretty pissed since he specifically told us not to sign our names. I was following directions for once, and look where it got me.

By junior year, I got it together and started to focus more on my studies. My parents were on my case more after a disastrous academic sophomore year. I began doing my homework and learning the material at home again. I was back up to Bs and As. Apparently, college was something that I needed to be mindful of, so it was important that I didn't take myself out of the game entirely. Between wrestling every day after school and even having my first girlfriend, Jackie, a dark-haired freshman who was taller than me by an inch or so, and incredibly smart beyond her years, I still managed to get solid grades. The exception was Latin, another mostly dead language. It reminded me of Hebrew and I pulled a fat C.

Since I pulled an A somehow in American History junior

year, I had the option of taking my first AP (Advanced Placement) class. It was AP Government, and I had the well-known Mr. Dooley as my teacher. Mr. Dooley was very animated in his classroom and made learning fun—somehow. I used to love Mr. Dooley's class since the course itself was taught at college level and I felt somewhat honored to be surrounded by most of the Asian population in my grade—clearly the upper echelon of academic excellence in Holmdel High School. Mr. Dooley was unlike any other teacher I had ever had as his sense of humor kept us laughing almost the whole way through. His Homer Simpson expressions and his random comedic improvisations kept us at least somewhat attentive. A tough task for me, but no other teacher had ever been more successful in keeping me engaged. His class was a nice break from the ineffective monotony of the mostly sequential auditory learning style unsuitable for the creative right-brained thinker, which was prevalent in the rest of my classes that year, and really every other year, including college. He would not only mention the lesson as stated in the text book and transfer it to the blackboard verbatim, but he would also actually abstract in an effort to relate a certain historical event or governmental concept to today's society. I needed more of this to keep me attentive during class, because without a big-picture analysis or understanding, it was difficult for me to process the information.

This is not to say that I was a perfect pupil in Mr. Dooley's class. As mentioned, my attention span and difficulty with the typical classroom was just as prominent inside his classroom. Oftentimes when I was seated and expected to remain in complete attention for the sake of a lecture I was stricken with an almost unbearable urge to get up and move around, almost as if to keep my brain alive. I have found, oddly enough, that if I am in motion, my ability to focus during a conversation or a lecture is drastically improved. Incidentally, I think they should put ADHD kids on treadmills during class. They will get more out of it.

One day, while sitting in AP Government class, the bell sounded to indicate the end of the period. Mr. Dooley, in an attempt to send me a hint, mentioned to the class, "The lesson of the day must have been especially interesting since BRIAN didn't get out of his seat and leave." I deserved the subtle remark as it was true that I would normally leave for about ten minutes a day and wander over to the commons to socialize with my friends in seventh period lunch. The reality of the situation was that I needed the break from sitting, as almost every kid with ADHD has trouble sitting still. I was retaining information, despite being fidgety. I pulled a B and never took notes. I couldn't take notes. Mr. Dooley even made a comment about how I never wrote anything down, yet still did "pretty well." Really, what I had to do was take the book home with me and work hard at self-instruction straight from the text. At my own pace was the only way it was going to get learned.

* * *

Mr. Dooley's was not the only teacher subject to my frequent departures, and oftentimes I'd even be walking around or away without even knowing I was in motion. At home, I'd sometimes be running up the stairs and my dad would say with some concern, but mostly fascination, in his voice, "Bri, do you even know where you are going?" I'd yell back, "NOPE," but never would I stop.

Later in life, I'd find myself walking in a group with no predetermined destination, when all of the sudden someone would yell out, "Brian!" I'd stop in my tracks and yell, "What?" Then I'd hear something along the lines of, "Where are we going?" I would look around and say, "No idea!" "But we are following you," they'd respond, to which I'd throw my hands up in bewilderment. "That was your first mistake!" That has happened to me on multiple occasions throughout almost every stage in my life. People need to stop following me just because I'm walking. Ask if you are unsure.

Luckily, the unbearable urge to get up and move around was provided its own outlet in wrestling practice after school, though even in the wrestling room there were days where my inattentiveness led me to some pretty uncomfortable situations. I remember one day in wrestling practice, Coach Mullen was teaching us new pin techniques. I was off in Bri Bri Land. I know now that if I was not focused as Mullen gave a physical demonstration of a new technique, there was no chance I was going to catch up when he verbally commanded us to drill. We all knew we were in big trouble if we were having trouble drilling. He would approach you as he brought the rest of the team to an abrupt halt and direct rest of the team to create a circumference around you until the move was performed correctly. I'll never forget the time he stood over me for forty-five minutes screaming directions in my face. The rest of the team could only watch as I made the same mistake repetitively. I remember wondering, *Why in the world I could not understand what he was saying?* That stung for a couple of days, but I got over it. My memory of it now is razor sharp: Mullin screaming some sort of foreign language at me whose sound made my eardrums quake and whose content was caught in some sort of echoing feedback loop.

Wrestling, overall, was a good experience for me, as it would instill in me a certain physical and emotional confidence that remains to this day. Despite my occasional mishaps due to inattention, Coach Mullin would bring forth in all of us a new personal peak in mental toughness. We could not possibly have reached this level without his relentless encouragement and, in some cases, without the embarrassment and physical pain he put us through. It was in the wrestling room where I was able to instill the willingness and wherewithal to stay tough and positive during the hard times I endured later in life.

We would run around the high school and middle school twice, the equivalent of about two miles, just to warm our muscles before practice. An extensive stretching session was followed by the actual beginning of practice, where Coach would enter the room and begin drilling. If we had performed poorly the night before in a match, or if he was just plain in a bad mood, drilling might be pushed back to make room for a grueling conditioning session usually involving "hit its," a variation of a military training technique where we would have to drop to the floor while simultaneously throwing our legs back into a *V* shape and get back up in a split second. Other times, we would form a line and run the perimeter of the auditorium, scaling up and down the top row seating and into the upper bleachers with our teammates on our backs.

*　*　*

I was expected to really make my mark in wrestling senior year. I was prepared in my own mind, and Coach's mind, for a full-time varsity position. I had earned my letter as a junior, though I spent a fair amount of time on junior varsity behind some of the seniors who had earned their spot. I was 2-1 early in the season and had demonstrated promise before breaking my wrist, for the second time (first time being freshman year), snowboarding at Hunter Mountain in the Catskills region of New York. I had tried to launch off a ten-foot jump with a reckless amount of momentum while attempting to grab the tail of my board in midair. The landing was misplaced, and I cracked my wrist in an attempt to soften the fall. It was very upsetting for me and disappointing for the team as I watched on the sidelines with a cast up to my elbow for the remainder of my season.

As the weather began to turn warm in early spring, and my last season of wrestling was behind me, I could not have been happier and more carefree. It was almost as if the inner disturbance of the past had completely dissipated. Of course, like most reflective individuals, there was much to think about as college became a reality.

Chapter 5
New Orleans

What better city for a new college student than New Orleans. With an economy that thrives on alcohol consumption and a legal system as backward as my scattered mind, I still do not know how that city can possibly be part of the United States. New Orleans was more like a third-world country to me, providing endless opportunities to live as reckless and free. So long as I didn't flunk out, which actually was a concern of mine going in, the next four years would be an immaculate firework display of pretty women, mind-numbing beverages, and funky music.

When I first arrived at Tulane University, my parents took me over to the ERC, or Educational Resources and Counseling Center. Apparently, my parents had gone through a lengthy process to qualify me as a special-needs student. It was the first I'd heard of it. We never really talked about it much. I think my parents didn't want me to think of myself that way, even if they knew there were some "unique" differences I possessed. I suppose the special-needs card helped me to get into Tulane, but I never gave it much thought. I was ADHD; big deal, right? Tulane was my reach school, but I guess having family as alumni and registering as a special-needs student was enough to get me in the door. I remember having to explain my sophomore year in my essay, and I suppose my SAT was just good enough, but not stellar by any means.

My first-semester course load consisted of Psych 101, Introduction to Politics, Thomas Jefferson and His Times (my freshman writing requirement), Spanish 101, and Leadership. I ended up dropping Leadership though; I told my dad I needed to focus more on my other courses. The truth was I felt outmatched in an interactive classroom of freshman peers. They were so articulate, and had such advanced vocabularies. I tried to voice my opinion at one point during the first class but could barely manage to piece together a sentence. I felt like I had some pretty good ideas in my head, but I found myself searching for words. I remember thinking that those kids were obviously much smarter than me, and I withdrew immediately.

I started thinking that maybe the honors dorm was not for me and I began to investigate the two more mainstream accommodations—Sharp and Monroe. I was not an honors student, anyway, but my friend Jay was, and we had chosen to be roommates. The non-honors dorms were livelier and much more fun than Butler. Those were the "cool" kids at Tulane. I remember thinking a lot of them were pretty jappy—that some of the girls were real Jewish American Princesses—but otherwise pretty cool. I was not used to having so many other Jews in my classes. About a third of Tulane's student body was Jewish.

I ended up staying in Butler with Jay, as I was already making friends there. I was beginning to enjoy the interesting individuals roaming the halls. I was living among would-be Ivy Leaguers who had decided that a full ride at Tulane might be a nice alternative. They were a great group of people, and we had the time of our lives at Butler that year.

From the beginning, Jay and I were exploring as usual. We would run up and down the stairwells introducing ourselves to random Butler occupants, while pretty much leaving our mark wherever we went. Amber and Robin were nice enough to leave blue markers outside their door for friends to leave notes on their miniature white boards. I wrote in somewhat-legible blue marker in gigantic letters, B-ROB, taking up the entire top half of the door. This was followed by three barely legible letters: "Jay." The first time I heard B-ROB was the night before at a fraternity party and I was digging it. B-ROB soon became its own self-manifesting phenomenon. At Tulane, I was B-ROB to most everyone who knew me. Later on, at Morgan Stanley, my colleague Sizwe coined the term, and it spread like wildfire within my department. I have never once introduced myself as B-ROB, but it sure stuck. I think the B-ROB persona even gave me a little leeway for some of the wild stunts I pulled and the overall outlandishness of my personality.

* * *

Weeks passed and our first college exams were upon us. I remember that our first writing assignment for Jefferson and His Times was due. I had a rough draft reflecting on the readings we covered. Since the class was both a history and a required English proficiency course, it was our professor's duty to improve our writing while teaching us the important historical perspective. He handed us our papers and dedicated the first half of the class to dissecting an anonymous example of what represented exactly how *not* to write an introductory paragraph. The professor was critical of the intro, as the thoughts were blasted on paper with no cohesive organization, but I was more interested in the brunette who was clearly checking me out from the other side of the table. Also, he was using my paper.

* * *

Jay and I used to receive calls almost every night from some fraternity trying to recruit us. We always made a dynamic team. One night we were invited to a party held by the Pi Kappa Alpha fraternity called PIKE. This fraternity epitomized the NYC cosmopolitan, obliterate-yourself party mentality of Tulane. These were the Northeast city kids who loved women in multiples, excessive quantities of drugs and alcohol, and embraced an I-don't-give-a-fuck attitude, all of which had major appeal to me. These kids were clearly capable of more mayhem than some of the other fraternities on Broadway (fraternity row). They would buy me shots at The Boot, the just-off-campus bar that they seemingly owned. I considered joining up, but something just didn't feel right.

It was their annual "Saturate" party, and I was having a grand old time. We were taking shots of Bacardi poured down blocks of ice chiseled with alcohol chutes from which we were expected to catch the liquid in our mouths. Later on, I was introduced to the "Vat," which is Tulane's version of traditional college "jungle juice" made with 190 proof Everclear. Of course, PIKE was always suspected of adding a little extra something to the mix to help the young ladies relax, but I didn't speculate.

I remember I found my way upstairs at some point and became part of an unfortunate standstill in the hallway. I was not having nearly as great of a time after the enthusiastic intensity of my initial arrival, and I was not sure why. Something about the way these people interacted with each other downright bothered me. I'll never forget when a Paris Hilton-type girl cut in front of me with unwavering entitlement as we were all waiting to fill our cups. The act did not affect me nearly as much as her character. I impulsively dumped whatever was left of my blood-red Vat over her artificially glowing blonde hair. It was pure artistic expression if you ask me, but her PIKE boyfriend didn't agree.

He was one of the upperclassmen, and therefore not one of the sophomores who were actively involved in recruitment. Once again, I was ushered off the premises, but this time, I was enraged. I recall standing across the street at the corner of where The Boot resided, screaming my lungs out for him to come fight me. A couple of the PIKEs who did know me came out and offered to buy me some shots if I would only go with them as some of the others explained to the upperclassman that they knew me and I was okay. Of course, I refused and kept hollering until the NOPD threatened to "slam my head into the concrete and beat it to a bloody pulp." That was the point where the people I arrived with, including Jay, decided it was time for me to move far away from Broadway, at least for the time being. I was eighteen and drunk out of my mind. My friends were laughing. It never feels like there are any real consequences when you're that age. They catch up eventually, though.

PIKE was clearly not for me, even though most who knew me probably would have thought differently. I made the decision not long afterward that the mainstream Tulane crown would not be a large part of my life, either. Jay never wanted to join a fraternity in the first place, but ended up pledging Alpha Tau Omega with me. There were a couple of other Jewish guys that fell off the mainstream bandwagon in ATO, which was originally founded as a Christian fraternity. When pledging began, I remember being relieved that I passed all my classes the semester prior. I ended first semester with a 2.7 GPA, with my best mark in Jefferson and His Times—a B. I guess my writing improved despite that dreadful first assignment. The professor told me at one point that it was clear to him that I understood the content of the readings, even with some of the poorer papers I handed in. It did take me a while to figure out how to organize my thoughts on paper. Later on in life my ideas would flow to paper with greater ease.

At the risk of putting ATO through any type of regulatory investigations, I will not go into detail about pledging and all the old anti-establishment ways of a younger Brian in Hebrew school, even though our chapter lost its charter a mere year and a half after I graduated in August of 2005. To sum up my time with pledging, I pissed off many of the older guys by refusing to partake in certain rituals the fraternity religiously abided by, while inviting as much pain and physical punishment as they could possibly administer. I gained respect as a badass with a high threshold for pain, even though I was clearly putting forth the bare minimum as far as most other organized activities were concerned. There were days when Jay and I would come home after a night of boozing and disconnect our phone, knowing full well we were supposed to be at "The House" early the next morning. We did what we wanted, for the most part.

* * *

By the time sophomore year swung by, I was living with a couple of ATOs in an off-campus apartment. Jay and our friend and Denny ended up living together in sophomore housing on campus. They were both a little offended, but the truth was I needed my own room off campus. One thing I had discovered in college was that I needed a lot of time to myself to keep my wandering mind in line. Truth is, in college at least, I always managed to offend, in some way or another, anybody who ever considered themselves to be my friend. I was flighty and disconnected while exploring all sorts of different social domains, never sticking around long enough in any one of them to get to know people the way I probably should have. I was afraid to get too close to people, and really didn't like socializing sober. Maybe, with the ADHD, I was afraid that if anyone knew me too well, they would realize I was not as cool or dynamic as I could appear initially, and that I would get anxious in conversations as I sometimes did because I wasn't always following. For this reason, I kept myself in constant movement and it allowed me to operate with a perpetual element of disconnectedness, something that I absolutely needed if I was going to function as one who is social at all. I always wondered how it was possible, for someone who intuitively feels like an extreme introvert, to exhibit such overt behavior.

* * *

Aside from my friends in the fraternity, I was friends with science geeks, liberal hippies, conservative Southerners, and yes, even some japs. Most Japs, like people in general, are cool once you get to know them. Others really are not. It always amazed me how almost everyone else was so one-dimensional in their thinking that they could never considering friendship with each other. About a month into sophomore year I could feel this very social dynamism and motivation dim ever so gradually. I never was able to rediscover my social motivation, at least not for a while. It must have seemed funny to a lot of people that I lived with three other ATOs while displaying such a low level of interest in the fraternity itself. My father always told me I was too independent for my own good.

I found myself reading much more than ever before. I was known to read books here and there, but I would never have been described as a bookworm. I am a slow reader as I must visualize what the author is telling me. It is like getting a sneak preview of what a movie based on the book would be like. By early sophomore year, and ever since, I have always read or studied a book of my choosing. I have always learned more through self-study than anything from a school curriculum, though I was absolutely intrigued by the subject of philosophy after I took the introductory course second semester freshman year. It was a broad introduction where we heard briefly from classical minds like Aristotle and Platos's Socrates and German philosopher Friedrich Nietzsche.

Philosophy struck me as very different from every other school subject I had ever encountered, even though it is ironically the oldest of all academic disciplines. For the many people who disregard philosophy as not necessary or even relevant, I wonder if they ever realized that every other subject in school is derived from philosophy, with economics and psychology paying major credence to their philosophical forebears.

True to my nature, I still did not read most of the assigned readings, but I was never more stimulated by school than I was by the simple idea that there were and are people like me who are willing to question every convention that stands before them—not to be a pain, but because they need proof in the form of mathematical language. Logic was that language to me. The philosophical mind is the mind of the true explorer. It is a documented fact that Einstein considered himself a philosopher first and a scientist second. I began to realize that everything I suspected in one way or another about human character and action was under consideration by some of the greatest thinkers of all time. Finally, I was able to appeal to the inner depths of my intellect. I was beginning to look at the way humanity operates in a very different light, as I fell deeper into an existential depression.

Nietzsche, for instance, wrote about the will to power that every person supposedly possesses, and being at a school like Tulane, where I was beginning to grow frustrated with the general character of the school's drone mentality, Nietzsche's words manifested into truth. I would contemplate the pressure to someday become a good Jewish boy and go to business school or law school, and I saw most of the people around me going through those very motions like robots. I began to see myself among a group of drones, so to speak, making contacts and networking, artificially communicating in order to serve their own selfish agendas. I'm not saying I was being fair to people with this mindset, but it was where I was at the time.

* * *

My perception of human behavior and motives was inching closer to cynical with each passing day. I began to fall into a void of subtle paranoia, which was further inflamed after a fight with a few of my high school friends. The summer after freshman year, only weeks before we were meant to travel back to New Orleans, someone decided to stash a small bag of marijuana in the glove compartment of my Volkswagen without asking my permission. If truth be told, at nineteen I probably would have let my friends ride with it if they kept it on their person, but someone instead chose to put the entire carload at risk, which consisted of the three of us: Jay, my old high school friend Tim, and me. It was a little past two in the morning on a lazy weekday night, when I made a right on a red light at the corner of Laurel Avenue and Route 35. I barely had time to straighten out the wheel before I saw the red, white, and blue flashing in my rear-view mirror.

The least that could happen, I thought to myself, was the cop would give me a ticket for turning right on red at an intersection that doesn't allow such a maneuver. The officer shined his light in my face and asked me for my license and registration. You see, due to the scarcity of actual crime in the cozy suburb of Holmdel, New Jersey, the Holmdel cops figure the best way to spend taxpayers' money is to focus nearly all of their efforts on breaking up house parties and pulling over every other kid with a baseball cap and a subwoofer in the back of their automobile. I pulled open my glove compartment and there it was, to both my surprise and the cop's—a bag of weed. All three of us were cuffed as he called for a K9 car to sniff out the rest of my vehicle. Part of me was confused, another part extremely angry, and still another part was somewhat thrilled by the events that unfolded at the end of what seemed to be a rather dull night.

We sat in the station and all I could think about was how someone had let us down, though I figured one of them would fess up eventually, thereby doing the right thing. As we left the station and climbed into our friend Adam's car, it was mostly silent until I lashed out at both of them at full volume, using the maximum capacity of my lungs.

"Why didn't one of you fess up? Do the right thing? You didn't even ask me if you could stash your drugs in my car!"

The days went on and I calmed myself down while assuring myself that whoever did it was only protecting himself in the police station for reasons only the law could make sense of, but that eventually he would come forth and protect his friends from what was obviously his own mistake. My girlfriend at the time, Allison, who was a Holmdel girl, eased me through the tough time by reinforcing to me everything would be fine, and that everyone would be friends again after it was over. Weeks went by, however, and the situation stayed stagnant. Nobody stepped up, and I was severely affected by it.

To be fair, Jay and I are still great friends almost fifteen years later. Tim and I haven't spoken in a decade or so. It was all adolescent idiocy. When you are an adult, it's easy to look back and recognize that we were just kids back then. We were being stupid. However, at the time, it was a big deal, and an unnecessary facet of my isolation at the time. Psychologists are on record about young people with ADHD having less ability to manage their emotions. They tend to feel things more intensely and it takes longer to come out of an emotion. Emotions can become dysregulated and cause trouble down the road.

* * *

When I came back to Tulane for sophomore year, with that summer's incident still fresh in my mind, I began to retreat into myself as I grew disheartened by the people I was spending time with. I formulated that if I could not trust my best friend, then I certainly could not trust anybody. Alcohol was still a large part of my life, but it began to lose its festive appeal. I needed it to escape as I gather I always have, but the party was over and the road to self-destructive behavior was downhill from here. I could not socialize without the aid of drugs and/or alcohol. Alcohol allowed me to escape while minimizing the anxiety of listening to people speak. The ATO house always welcomed those who wished to intoxicate themselves with no obligation to speak or be social. Some days I would go to The Boot and grab a seat on the raised platform in the back and watch the mass of people swaying back and forth like a drunken wave pool. I could sit there for hours as the real-time image in front of me played with dazzling clarity and overwhelming intensity. What is all this trying to tell me? What is happening that I can no longer play their game as I taught myself to in high school? Had I taught myself anything? No, not really.

* * *

Near the end of first semester sophomore year my friend Jeff and I took a drunken roller coaster ride at five in the morning over to the French Quarter. I always said that driving drunk in New Orleans was like bowling with those blue inflatable bumpers on the sides of the lane. The luxurious wide lanes of St. Charles Avenue made it easy to swerve and recover without contact with any inanimate objects.

We caused a ruckus at the Royal Sonesta Hotel on Bourbon Street, ripping pictures of the walls and setting off multiple alarms. We would have gotten away with it, but we decided after our exit that an encore performance was necessary. This time, the security guards were waiting for us and picked up our scent with impressive rapidity once we deserted the scene of our shenanigans. I recall trying to fight through the handcuffs they had managed to strap on our wrists. We ended up in New Orleans Parish County Jail for a solid fourteen-hour stay.

They took our mug shots soon after we entered the county jail, at which point I gave the camera the middle finger. Once again, the NOPD threatened my life, but I survived. I still have that picture somewhere. Next thing we knew, the sun had risen—or, at least, it was safe to assume so, being that there were no windows in our initial holding cells. We were soon ushered into another room down a long corridor and ordered to hand in our clothes and valuables in exchange for a set of Halloween-orange New Orleans Parish prison apparel.

At that point, we were ordered to strip to our underwear. As Jeff and I stood in a line with approximately thirty other individuals, prison guards scanned our bodies in search of any type of smuggled weapons or other prohibited items. Luckily, for obvious reasons, it was a mass scan rather than the type of individual body search experienced in airport security. After all, we were merely criminals, not international travelers. In any case, the guards did not do a very good job, as Jeff and I were almost immediately offered a hit from a joint by one of the young black individuals to our right. While we both refused, I could not help but feel the slightest sense of admiration for such a bold and ironic move on his part, though clearly it was quite stupid at the same time. Incidentally, it is said that between 25 percent and 40 percent of US criminals in the prison system have ADHD (this, according to the ADDA, or Attention Deficit Disorder Association). I was home!

Hours passed, and we were escorted to another section of the prison, where we ended up spending the majority of our stay. The large room had a sort of community feel to it with a large open area in the center, where the criminals could walk around and even socialize with one another. Jeff and I had entered just as everyone was asked to return to their cells, at which point we were both split up and introduced to our roommates for the time being. I looked over at yet another young African American, representative in my mind as the product of a city whose Old South tradition in some way succeeded in repressing the African American community. The overwhelming dichotomy between the rich and the poor in New Orleans is so drastic that the inevitability of high-level criminal activity is embedded as a mere function of an antiquated system. To me, as I sat there in a cell with a man who could be a first-degree murderer for all I knew, New Orleans being in constant competition for murder capital of the country, I merely saw him as human; no different from myself, as we sported the same orange clothes.

I looked at him and said, "What's up?"

He looked back at me and uttered the same sentiment.

"What's up?"

And that was that.

I spent the remaining hours in another chamber with a new group of about thirty people in the confines of a much smaller area than the initial mass holding cell, and this time there was a solid door rather than bars between us and our freedom. We sat there amid a nasty stench, with air as thick as gaseous ether, waiting for our names to be called. I suppose I deserved all of it. Luckily, my friend Denny had bailed me out and drove me home in his Saturn. I spent the duration of the car ride home not thinking about what I had done or how I had ended up in that situation, but rather which bars I was going to hit that night and wondering if Jeff was going to make it out in time to come with. I was not fazed, and furthermore, not even scared the least bit at any point during the entire experience. At Tulane, this was almost commonplace, as I can think of numerous students aside from myself spending a night in jail for underage drinking, which was the most unlikely offense to get busted for in a city like New Orleans—or public urination, which is even more prevalent. The list goes on.

When it came to our day in court, Jeff and I got off with a slap on the wrist thanks to Freddy King, the Tulane Law School–educated attorney who is kind enough to lend his services, for a meager $250 fee, to any Tulane student that finds him or herself in trouble, assuming you didn't kill anyone. Tulane lore has it that if you do kill someone, it will cost you one thousand dollars.

As for me and the less-than-healthy psychology that led me to such destructive behavior, I suppose part of it was a manifestation of a certain anti-authority attitude I have always carried with me. I never meant any harm to any other human being, but there was no denying that sophomore year I was certainly a risk to myself. I was frustrated by the loss of my best friend and, furthermore, was struggling academically while simultaneously immersing myself in a very philosophical and borderline paranoid mindset. My mind was distractible and was having trouble connecting meaning to the outside world. I was bitter and relied heavily upon alcohol to socialize. I needed help.

Chapter 6
ADHD Girlfriend

By second semester sophomore year, I was downright angry and paranoid. In classes I still had no capacity to focus. Words carried sound but no meaning and the sentences on the chalk board sometimes had a kaleidoscope-like effect on my eyes, but one without any aesthetic appeal. I used to walk around with gigantic headphones that looked like black plastic ear muffs. They would connect to my Sony Discman with a thick three-foot cable manufactured for home stereo systems. This was about a year before I picked up a first-edition iPod, which had come out in 2001. Elizabeth, a girl that lived around the corner from our four-room bungalow apartment in what some of my friends and I called the "Jap House," told me that she couldn't believe she was friends with the kid who walks around with headphones like that on.

I used to go to class in sweatpants or pajama pants as if they were my part of my school uniform. The only time I could be seen in respectable apparel would be around laundry time, when all of my most comfortable articles of clothing were vile. I could only clean my clothes with Tide Free, or else my skin would get irritated. Oftentimes I would walk into my critical thinking class (Logic 100) with my baby-soft black Burton sweatshirt hooded over my enormous black headphones and sit in the back as usual. I didn't utter a word for weeks until the topic of the day was the validation of authority through logistical analysis. My periscope was officially up. I cannot remember what I said so angrily and "poignantly" (as I was later told) to my instructor, as I knew he was incorrect, or at least not presenting the full picture, but apparently for the first time, someone took notice in a big way.

* * *

Her name was Molly Shire and she had emotional x-ray vision. She could feel my pain, somehow. She would turn around randomly and smile at me in class. Other times I'd catch her following me down the hallways in the Newcomb College building. But why? I was clearly not one of the mainstream preppy boys she had been known to rally around, and I was not very pleasant to her the couple of times I saw her at The Boot or Ms. Mae's on Napoleon Avenue. One day I essentially told her to get lost and that there was no saving me.

The first time we spent time together outside of philosophy class was the night I gladly accepted her invitation to go for a midnight stroll after a drunken night at The Boot. We walked for hours, first down the lemony-lit Audubon Drive, then past a row of beautiful New Orleans–style houses, and then we cut over to the Tulane Green Wave baseball diamond, where we had our first kiss in center field. The whole time she was smiling and laughing and squeaking. "ROOOBINSOOON!" she would yell. "Step BOY Step!" And then she would start dancing to the songs in her head. *This girl is as crazy as me,* I remember thinking. She was truly out of her mind, and I understood it completely.

During finals week, she jittered her way to my apartment as I was halfway through the twelve-page philosophy paper due the next morning. I had only begun the paper a few hours prior, but play time took precedence over work time.

We had chemistry, that's for sure. I could tell it had the makings of some serious atomic waves down the line, but it didn't matter. I swung my feet on her lap as she sat on my bed to try and get a rise out of her. I knew enough after being with her the last time that bare feet made her squeamish. She instantly took a liking to my feet though, and even took notice of the way my middle toe was longer than my big toe. She then took my hands into hers and pointed out that my fingers were those of a surgeon. *My father is a surgeon,* I thought, as I shook up a sealed bottle of Schweppes Ginger Ale and sprayed her with a blast of fizzy white pop. She laughed and popped her hood up as if to say "uncle." We spent the next few hours laughing like little kids; all the while, my paper remained unwritten. The sun rose and she danced her way back to Sharp Hall on the other side of campus.

That summer we spoke on the phone every other night. I was taking a biology class at Seton Hall University, marking the beginning of a struggle with a pre-medical curriculum. I'm not sure what it was that possessed me to take calculus, chemistry, and physics the first semester back at Tulane as a junior, but things were going to change and I vowed to take school very seriously. The developing mind of someone with ADHD has the tendency to set a goal and attempt to make it happen in a fury. Taking those three classes was impulsive and ultimately self-defeating, but you couldn't tell me that at the time. I was convinced that the only reason I had been a less-than-stellar pupil for so long was because I was lazy. This was the consensus of my teachers and even my parents. I had underachieved from the fifth grade through sophomore year in college. I was content with their perception. Underachievement as a description for someone implies a certain amount of unrealized potential. It was much better in my eyes to be underachieving than to be labeled as "doing the best he can." I dreamed that pre-med would be cake if I paid attention in class and studied hard. What did it matter that I had never taken a high school physics class or a pre-calculus class and had never taken any of the prerequisites? I didn't have time for that.

Molly came to the library to visit me one evening as I was staring blankly at Chapter One in my chemistry textbook. My new and improved attitude regarding paying attention in class was proving to be a futile effort. Paying attention was not a choice, I soon determined, and I resorted to self-study as I spent each class on a new adventure in Bri Bri Land. This time, however, self-study wasn't working. Why couldn't I do it like the others? I was putting in the same effort in the library every day, if not more, and it just wasn't happening for me. I could not process information like I had in the other subjects, especially in an educational environment. It was really upsetting and I was starting to feel like the architect of my own inevitable failure.

Molly could see the anguish on my face as the chemical equations I was attempting to learn burned my eyes. She popped a blue-colored pill in my mouth and told me, "Here, try this."

By that time, Adderall was being passed around on most college campuses like Skittles. I had long ago given up on medicine to help tame my ADHD, but this stuff was different. My thoughts began to flow like water and I could stare at a textbook for hours without fatiguing. One myth about Adderall: It does not make one smarter. It simply helps you sit in a chair for hours while a yearning to consume information. Many people have told me that while it does help you sit there for hours, your memory of what you were focusing on depletes the next day. I can attest to this was well. Despite all the studying I was doing, I wasn't learning the material very well. My tenuous grasp of simple algebra did not help me on my first physics exam, on which I scored a dismal 15 percent. Meanwhile, I simply could not juggle chemistry and calculus on top of my intermediate-level philosophy classes. My frustration grew as my relationship with Molly became more serious. It has always been in my nature to impulsively take on more than I can handle. Part of this stems from the impulsiveness of ADHD, but the rest comes from always wanting and desiring things at that moment, also an ADHD trait.

I recall spending a weekend with my parents in early fall, first semester junior year, in Arizona. My parents were there to enjoy the mountainous scenery and do some golfing, but they were happy nonetheless to accommodate their stressed-out son. My dad and I sat down and plowed through five hours of physics, of which the first couple of hours consisted of a basic rehash of algebra. The concepts involved in physics were not a problem for me; I simply couldn't do the math. It was always very frustrating to me that I felt I could always manage an intuitive grasp of scientific concepts but I simply lacked the ability to calculate numbers. I later learned that this sort of thing is typical for a visual thinker like me. I am able to visualize concepts with depth, but oftentimes two plus two would equal five after overanalyzing. I felt so stupid. Molly would reassure me time and time again that I was not dumb, which only intensified my embarrassment at my substandard grades. I used to wonder when she was going to realize that I was a complete fraud. My plan was in ruins as finals came around. All the studying I did yielded a mere 2.5 GPA for the semester. I managed a C in physics, a B in chemistry, and a Withdrawal from calculus.

The next semester, in typical nonsequential form, I decided I was ready to take genetics in front of its prerequisite, Cell Biology 101. For some reason, the online system let me enroll in this class. My decision probably should have been flagged, but I slipped through. It was a dumb move. If rote memorization and the commitment to raw detail coupled with neglect of a big-picture perspective is my weakness, then taking genetics at that time was possibly an error on my part. I came through with a C- while digging myself into an even deeper hole. My grade point average plummeted to 2.4 from 2.7 by the end of junior year, yet I continued to study pre-med. I made the decision that the Universidad de Guadalajara would be my future medical school as all the American medical schools had been more than ruled out by my own incapacity to learn. It is one thing, as I touched upon earlier, to walk through life with the comfort of knowing that there was always unrealized potential to tap. But it is a completely different situation when one tires themselves out through tortuous preparation, only to fail in the end.

Molly and I were in another realm of depth and intensity in our mutual infatuation from the beginning. It was more than either of us could handle in college at the time. Molly lived with three of her friends no more than a block from me. Her charisma, along with her high-voltage personality, made her not only popular, but a leader. She was not like the rest of the Tulane girls that followed her. For one, she did not have an eating disorder, which really made her stand out among the in crowd of Tulane socialites, at least in my eyes. Her dedication to yoga kept her in great shape. She was a bearer of sage advice and a lover of all that was fun and exciting. She was also lost in a world of superficiality and vanity, and she knew it didn't suit her despite her irrefutable ability to take center stage. The life

I had pledged to junior year as an introverted pre-med student added up to a proposition of stunning polarity as we both retreated into our relationship while the rest of the world stayed its course. Molly used to say, in true Shakespearean form, that "love is the sweetest of dreams and the worst of nightmares." I could relate to the nightmare element. Together, we fought the peer pressure her friends exerted in heavy doses to party with them and the time invested in my own seemingly futile effort to succeed in my classes. Yet, we loved each other, as much as two college students could conceive of love.

We ended up taking numerous weekend trips to get away from it all. There was the time we crossed through the barren yellow of Mississippi into Alabama, only to stop at the official motel of the USS *Alabama* Battleship Memorial Park in Mobile. The motel was like any other motel in the nation, except for the giant Navy battleship docked right outside. Another time we took a trip to Houston to catch a country music concert at Minute Maid Park, which was Enron Field before the awful accounting scandal. We used our fake IDs to get in since the bars weren't carding inside. I drank like a fish to drown out the inbred sound of a musical genre I was still far from accepting at the time. She took the first leg of the ride home while I sobered up. It marked one of the very few times she was allowed to drive. It just was not worth it for me to drive underage and under the influence in a state that thrives on rodeos and capital punishment.

We were about fifty miles outside Houston when Molly decided to drive in the left lane of the two-way street. She swerved out of the way of an oncoming car and hit the brakes and we hydroplaned off a four-foot launching pad of uneven landscape on the muddy shoulder of the right side of the road and glided into an unassuming telephone pole. The giant VW emblem met a violent end, but luckily, we both emerged unharmed. We flew home compliments of Molly's generous father the next day.

Molly and I ended as a couple in September, when she went off to Prague for the fall semester of her last year in college and I went to Shanghai, China, as a college grad in an international internship program. Both of us needed to get away from New Orleans for a while—and maybe from each other. I'll always be indebted to Molly for the impact she had on me at the time.

We were two kids with ADHD who understood each other very well, and she helped me believe in my mental abilities when I couldn't think of any reason to do so.

I had dropped pre-med second semester senior year with only two classes remaining, Physics 2 and Chemistry 2, which I had failed once before. Somehow, I found my way through Organic Chemistry 1 and 2 with a D and a B respectively. Most of my 2005 peers graduated that spring; I graduated a few months later in August with a Bachelor of Arts in Philosophy following the long-anticipated completion of calculus.

Chapter 7
Vision Asia

Molly and I took an anthropology class, Modern Chinese Society, in the spring semester of my senior year, which was her junior year. Molly had always embraced Eastern philosophy and practiced yoga on an almost daily basis. She was very talented and even encouraged me to take Kung Fu classes, where I eventually earned my blue belt. Our class was taught by a Miss Du, who had written a book based on her extensive experience in the cultural transformation China had undergone since the post-Mao communist regime. While significant change had already transpired in China long before its widespread coverage in the United States, my decision to travel to Shanghai was cutting-edge. There is always a significant lag between the occurrence of major change and the mass recognition of such change, especially in this country.

Most of what I knew about China was derived from martial arts movies. My all-time favorite was the aesthetically dazzling and philosophically inspired *Hero*. It remains tied with *Gladiator*. *Hero* depicts a character whose family was slaughtered by the emperor's Imperial Army on its road to a unified China. At the time, China was fractioned into sovereign providences, though the power of the emperor's army was growing exponentially despite the resistance of the land. The main character swore revenge and drew up an elaborate plan to situate himself close to the emperor, disguised as a loyal follower. The hero was the only martial artist in the land with the ability to execute the type of deadly attack necessary to dethrone and assassinate the emperor, and by the time the emperor realized his mistake, the pieces were already in checkmate. The hero did not follow through with his plan because he looked into the king's heart and was reminded of a friend he had met along the way whose notion of "our land" rang true in his soul for the first time. Suddenly, unification became the roadway to a glorious future for the Chinese people, per his untimely revelation. The hero died for his efforts in the face of a compassionate, yet pragmatic emperor.

Like the United States after it, a country that stands for unity while paying homage to its parts will ultimately reap the benefits of a global leadership in thought and influence. General Sun Zhu, author of the internationally known book *The Art of War,* advocated that one must know his enemy to conquer, while one must know oneself in order to be unconquerable. A country must know itself and its enemy, as this very principle is universally applicable. To know themselves, our schools must recognize the intelligence of those lateral thinkers within whose learning style varies from those of the norm set by the school system.

In the utilitarian point of view of our nation's school system, the education that maximizes the number of students who benefit from a curriculum geared toward the predominant a learning style are ultimately responsible for minimizing the potential of students with different cognitive styles. As it follows, maximizing the mass of students who benefit from our country's educational system doesn't maximize the good for society. History has proven repeatedly that it is the mind of just one individual whose independent ideas prove to be the catalyst of cultural or scientific progression. We must know ourselves to reverse this trend of neglecting students made vulnerable by this system, and we must know our enemy in the form of that which stands in the way of competing on the global stage of intellectual progress.

* * *

When I first arrived at Shanghai Pudong Airport, the first thing I noticed in this great land of economic and scientific innovation was the foreign pictographic symbols of the Chinese language. I silently prayed that the mass influx of Westernization and transformation in this country would give way to English subtitles on street signs, at least in Shanghai, the thought leader in Chinese economic pioneerism. As we disembarked, the stewardesses informed us where we could pick up our baggage. Of course, my mind was elsewhere and the words deflected off my skull like ping pong balls. I spent a good hour trying to locate my baggage after many failed attempts to engage in conversation with some of the baggage handlers. Finally, I saw three red pieces of luggage sitting by their lonesome that looked familiar. I grabbed them and spent another incalculable length of time finding David, the director of Abroad China, the international internship program. He introduced himself as we packed his car up in anticipation of the two-hour crawl through traffic into the heart of Shanghai.

As early evening gave way to night, I was genuinely exhausted by the fourteen hours of flying I had just endured. I recall being hypnotized by the electronic map that we each had on the back of the headrest in front of us. While everyone else was watching *Seinfeld* or Brad Pitt and Angelina Jolie as Mr. and Mrs. Smith on their personal screens, I watched in awe as we flew over the North Pole before we dipped down through Russia, Mongolia, and then China. There were little icicles forming on the windows as we rounded the top of the globe and now there were blindingly exuberant neon lights keeping me awake as we passed through the outer circumference of the famous Pu Xi (East) region of Shanghai.

Shanghai is truly a sight in the nighttime, as most of the major buildings are lit up in celebration of their occupants as the thriving economic drivers of a newly emerging city amid one of the grandest economic revolutions in world history. Everything was changing before my very eyes, and the United States was still a good year away from fully appreciating the magnitude of the seismic shift in global influence that lay ahead. Picture a collection of highly energetic molecules aggregating in the early phases of a big bang, or on a simpler note, picture yourself in the stands as a high school freshman named LeBron James lights a gym up with forty points in little-known Akron, Ohio. These were the early phases of a global phenomenon.

That first night we sat down and enjoyed a traditional Szechuan dinner complete with spicy peanut chicken, thinly sliced pork, dumpling soup, and for dessert, a community bowl of oversized tapioca balls drowned in warm, sugary water. To my left were Zach and Tiffany, a pair of thirty-year-olds who had enrolled in the same program. Tiffany was fresh out of the Georgetown University MBA program while Zach was a graduate of the Wharton Business School at the University of Pennsylvania with five years of investment banking under his belt. They were newly wed as of the previous July, and with Zach being Cantonese and Tiffany being a blonde Midwesterner from Indiana, they were certainly an interesting duo from the start.

To my right was Angela, a quiet Chinese girl from Los Angeles with a cool demeanor and an anxious desire to please. She sat quietly as David, our program director, enlightened us with such details as to where we could find phone cards to call home, the proper attire for our internships, as well the current yuan-to-dollar currency exchange ratio, which was somewhere around 8:1.

Following dinner, David showed Angela and me to the hotel that would be our home for the next three months. The Xinyu Hotel was approximately a twenty-minute subway ride to People's Square and thirty-minute subway ride from the famous tree-lined French Concession of Shanghai. It boasted a friendly staff with a nicely maintained lobby and a whorehouse on the top level. The elevators also operated with excruciating slothfulness. For a city that seemed to be riding a bolt of lightning to the frontier of technological innovation, how could an elevator function with such disregard for the times? Our rooms were no less retro with their neon-yellow bed covers and bright-pink desk lamps; it felt like a Holiday Inn crossed with a flamboyant expression of utilitarianism. And boy, was it hot, inside and out! Shanghai in early September was as offensively humid as New Orleans.

I recall lying there that first night, having not seen Molly since she left Tulane after the first summer session of classes had ended in early July, and thinking that times certainly were changing unrecognizably. Part of me embraced this idea, as I have always chased after exotic new experiences, but there was something about the blinding yellow of my bed sheet that sent me off to sleep with an unwavering sense of depression.

The next morning I was up by eight with my Nike Air Maxes laced up tight for what I could feel was going to be a very long walk. I knew nothing about the geography of Shanghai aside from its signature television tower that looks more like a radioactive rocket ship ready to take off for the planet Techno Rave. Dating back to as early as I can remember, with emphasis on the numerous hours I used to spend exploring the wilderness of Holmdel and Toms River, I have never hesitated to point myself in a seemingly arbitrary direction with nothing but self-guided instinct as my compass. Typical ADHD lack of planning eventually evolves into an adapted sense for situating yourself after getting lost. My destination was the waterfront, where the TV tower would inevitably be found, and all I had with me was my honed spatial intuition for direction. I found myself walking down roads whose names I could not pronounce even with the English subtitles. I remember stopping for a cold bottle of green tea at a convenience store. The cost was three yuan, or close to forty cents. After about a mile and a half of walking, I saw what struck me as a faint outline of the television tower I had only seen in pictures on the Internet. Judging by the fleeting vista of tall buildings, and more importantly, the TV tower in the distance, and my own relative geometric positioning, there was clearly hours of undiscovered city to cover.

I walked past neighborhood after neighborhood of the most efficient-looking apartment complexes, many under some phase of construction. The rural Chinese were moving to Shanghai and its surrounding areas in search of a more prosperous existence. I found myself at one point on a dirt-paved alleyway that might as well have been three hundred years back in time as I passed by men selling live chickens from cages and families tending to their stock of live snakes and other unidentifiable river specialties. These spectacles were getting rarer; those tending to a new shipment of the latest pirated DVD to hit the market were a more common sight in the tech-savvy world of Shanghai consumerism.

Old neighborhoods like the one I found on my first day are truly the hidden gems of a rapidly Westernizing city whose ancient Chinese culture has dissipated into the thick cloud of industrial smog that monopolizes the air passages of inexperienced tourists. Two hours later, I found myself on the Huang Pu riverfront gazing toward the western portion (Pu Dong) of Shanghai. Present was the ever-multiplying financial district, which crowded around the colossal Jin Mao Tower, the tallest and most modern building in Shanghai at the time. It reminded me of the way the Empire State building looks nestled among the hundred or so other smaller buildings in New York City, as the way one could only view it across the Hudson River from New Jersey. Finally, the most uniquely designed television tower on earth, with its syringe-like body beaded with two massively rotund neon balls, as only the Chinese could draw up, stood before my very eyes like an overgrown tripod on acid.

I taxied it back to the hotel since there was no plausible method of retracing my steps. It is one thing to point yourself in the general direction of a giant backdrop and strut your way through an urban obstacle course of random confusion. It is an entirely different scenario to even attempt to reverse the process. It is like anything else; the more nonlinear an approach utilized to reach a goal, the more chaotic that process becomes until you hit the point of irreversibility. This is universal entropy at its finest, and hence, my justification for hailing a taxi. Also, I was plain beat.

The Shanghai taxis were lined with white seat covers for an extra touch of sophistication as one is driven through this utter freak of a city. If a passenger does not know the Chinese language, he better have a card with a written address for the driver to read. Of the hundreds of taxis taken in my four months living in Shanghai, I can only count one time where my driver could manage more than a "Hello." They were truly their own breed; with their thermoses filled with loose-leaved green tea and their routine near-death collisions around every bend, the Shanghai taxi drivers made New York taxi drivers seem laid back.

A couple of nights later, the program set up a dragon boat tour down the Huang Pu River for the whole group of Abroad China interns. It was that very night that I met Ahmad Motadi, the Saudi-born Sheik of Miami whose most recent residence was in Lebanon. I could tell right away that Ahmad and I were going to be spending a lot of time together. For starters, we figured out quickly that he was my next-door neighbor back at the hotel, and he could clearly hold his own in the drinking department as well, judging by the way he guzzled his first Tsingtao beer.

The boat docked, and we hit the town. First it was the white lights and glitziness of Tong Ren Lu (*Lu* is "road" in Mandarin). Tong Ren Lu was just down the road from the Shanghai Ritz-Carlton and a short walk from the newly constructed Shanghai International Convention Center, where businesspeople flock to introduce their latest products into the China market. Ahmad and I took three shots of Jameson whiskey and stood as two lone gunmen since the last of the interns had long ago said their goodnights and farewells. We hopped in a taxi and ended up on Chu Lu Lu, where we were told we would find the last of the open bars. Within minutes we found ourselves slumped over on bar stools playing Connect Four with the lady bartenders, this alongside a drunk English expatriate and his lovely Shanghainese girlfriend. We laughed endlessly as I schooled the bartender in the game and tossed back more whiskey until we blacked out. I think...

* * *

After an interesting weekend, it was time to get ready to work. Upon acceptance to the program, Abroad China sent my résumé to several Chinese companies looking for English-speaking interns. Jamie Gwyn, managing director of his own consulting company, Vision Asia, happened to be a Louisiana State University graduate and jumped at the chance for a Tulane kid to work among his entirely Chinese staff. Jamie had arrived in Shanghai in 1999 under the pretense that he would perform potato logistics for Frito-Lay. He recognized potential in a growing, though very immature, Shanghai market when he arrived and opened his own shop. When I arrived September 2005, Vision Asia was in the process of being merged into the larger and more knowledgeable Spire Research and Consulting. I realized immediately that the fledgling enterprise had potential, but didn't quite have the expertise it might have needed to be a bigger player.

I walked in with Tiffany, who had also been selected by Vision Asia via Abroad China, as a very amiable and somewhat nervous Belinda Yu greeted us. Belinda was born in Beijing and spoke English with an Australian accent. She and the rest of the Vision Asia work force were especially cheery and welcoming. In Shanghai, they were putting forth their best effort to acclimate themselves toward a Westernized model of business, and employing true-blooded Americans was a sign of prestige and dominance. My greatest tangible asset in Shanghai was not a liberal arts degree, but the mere fact that I could speak English in a rapidly adapting Chinese business world. Tiffany and I were highly regarded instantly.

After Belinda provided us with a brief overview of what was expected from us, Jamie walked through the glass door of the conference room and introduced himself. Jamie was five feet, five inches tall at most, about average among Chinese males, but on the short end of the spectrum by American standards. I had a solid four inches on Jamie, while Tiffany downright towered at six feet. He told us right away about how exciting a time it was to be experiencing Shanghai, and he couldn't have been more right. I could feel the city's undercurrent of energy and growth with every stride. It was amazing to me how Jamie or any Western entrepreneur could own and operate a company in China and not know more than a couple of sentences of Mandarin. Even in their own country, a Chinese person must learn to speak the language of the American businessperson if they have any aspirations of being more than a farming peasant or a lowly urban service provider.

Following Jamie's introduction, we took a walk through the French Concession and sat for a fancy Szechuan lunch. All the staples of a Westernized Chinese food takeout meal were present as we nibbled on Kung Pao chicken and spare ribs. Things became interesting however, when the waiter brought out frog legs, which, of course, I tried. My philosophy on food is I will try anything at all if it is edible—once. After the frog legs, we were all enticed by a fried jelly fish, though the most unexpected dish of the afternoon appeared in the form of a white tofu-like substance in a black cauldron over a small flame. The flame was responsible for gently boiling a dark red liquid in which the white cubes were submerged. Instinctively, I reached for a piece of what I thought was tofu and slid it into my mouth, grinned, and swallowed. Oscar, Jamie's right-hand man, wanted to know right away how I had "enjoyed the taste of boiled pig's blood." I told him I enjoyed it very much and would like some more.

* * *

As the weeks passed, I grew weary of my job. I was under Oscar's supervision and I was expected to create a PowerPoint presentation based upon some of the research the other Chinese employees had gathered for the Shanghai market for document management. Oscar's English was so poor and his directions so imprecise that I had supposedly been working for two weeks on a project whose purpose was lost somewhere in the Pacific Ocean between Hawaii and Japan. While it was true that I had not the slightest idea of the directions Oscar had given me, my ability to pick up on the conceptual structure enabled me to quickly figure out his less-than-cogent methodology. The research I was handed pertaining to Fuji Xerox printer/fax machine lineup lacked real insight, as it consisted of information that any individual could easily extract from the company's website in a matter of twenty minutes. I was operating at a standstill until Jamie called me into his office sometime in late September and suggested that Oscar and I were perhaps not sharing a productive working relationship. In my mind, if Oscar truly had a problem, he needed to take it up with me personally. In the US, if two men have a problem with each other, they resolve it face to face. Jamie agreed with a somewhat genuine gesture of affirmation, though he was not overwhelmingly moved.

The next day, I was moved over to the sales team, where poor Tiffany had been cold-calling virtually every Chinese company with a Shanghai, Beijing, or Hong Kong area code to drum up business. The goal was to obtain the address of a company's head of marketing and send them a packet of information regarding the glorious things Vision Asia could do for them. While I was not really enjoying myself with my PowerPoint, sales was a different animal. It required short, consecutive bursts of energy. After a battery of calls, I managed to get the CFO of Sony Asia on the line and made an appointment for him to meet with Jamie. The joy of it all rushed to my head at once and I felt like I was floating when I stood to announce it. It was really cool at the time, but I didn't have it together all the way. They say that people with ADHD don't have the capacity to stick with things. They may start something with enthusiasm, but don't follow through after the novelty wears off. This was certainly my case.

My priorities didn't line up with being an adult with a job. Shanghai to me was just another playground and would pick up nicely where I left off at Tulane. Bourbon Street Hand Grenades and Jack and Cokes became blueberry mojitos and Chivas Regal on the rocks as Ahmad and I came home to the Xinyu lit up like a full Shanghai moon every night. Our favorite place to rendezvous was the internationally heralded Bar Rouge, which was situated right on the Bund with the most fantastic view of Pu Dong in all of Shanghai. We would get blitzed on the rooftop of a gorgeous seven-floor building with a muscular stone façade among a crowd of incredibly good-looking Western expats who did not think twice about paying five times the going rate for a beer in Shanghai as long they were able to enjoy it in the city's most elite party scene. I recall vividly, as I open the media player in my mind, the blazing electricity of the Shanghai (Pu Dong) skyline as viewed from the Bar Rouge patio at night. The eccentric neon colors would flash rhythmically throughout the night as if they were begging for the rest of the world to start paying close attention. I would sit in a hypnotic trance as the lights tickled the inner sensory mainframe of my mind with sharp potency. The flapping of the red and yellow Chinese flag above me would signal my subconscious with the high-frequency anticipatory vibrations of a new era.

Back at work, the excitement was building up for the Chinese Moon Festival on the first week of October. Moon cakes, which are best described as disc-shaped coffee cakes offered in a vast array of interesting flavors, such as red bean or egg yolk, were as abundant as Skittles and Milky Way bars around Halloween in the States. Since the holiday allowed for an extended weekend, I took the opportunity to secure a ticket to Prague to see Molly. My mother is really a wiz with some things, including the optimal usage of frequent flier miles. Somehow, she managed to get me on a flight. Ahmad and Angela were helping me pack my red carry-on luggage when Angela took a quick glance at my passport. Ten minutes before I was scheduled to leave for the airport, she announced that my Chinese visa was only single-entry. The three of us debated this new revelation for some time before I decided that I would just have to deal with the problem at the Chinese Embassy in Prague.

I have been described as reckless many times, and this was one of those times where I could certainly understand such an assessment. When it comes to red tape and meaningless regulation, I have been known to be unashamedly noncompliant. I wasn't a terrorist or a spy, so that's all that ought to matter. Once I'm in motion, there is no derailing my movement. My flight took off that night from Shanghai Pudong Airport.

I watched the digital map as we flew northwest from Shanghai through Beijing and then Mongolia. I fell asleep around the time the plane began to point due west over Russia. When I awakened, my vision was instantly drawn to the lights below, which according to the map was the city of Warsaw. Russia soon transitioned into Eastern Europe as we flew against the earth's rotation and faster than the rising sun behind us. When we landed in Paris, it was still a couple of hours before daylight. I had never been to France and would have loved to stay and check it out, but I was already late for another flight. When we walked off the plane I flashed my passport to the French officers as they were busy giving a Chinese traveler from my flight a hard time. They searched through his entire luggage while, to my surprise, the Chinese traveler voiced a calm but stern protest at the injustice. He told the officers that he would only show respect if they respected him in turn. Since I was in constant motion, it was simple to process the entire conversation.

We were on our way to Prague when I engaged in a short conversation with the gentleman sitting next to me. As an English-speaking American, he felt somewhat foreign to me, having just taken off from Paris and before that Shanghai.

He told me his company sends him all over Europe to handle factory integrations. He didn't offer any more details, but he did mention that he missed his family very much. I thought of my family too. My mom had expressed over one of my last dinners with my family before leaving for Shanghai that she didn't think I was coming back. As we landed in Prague, I wondered the same thing. I had been struggling to find a suitable fit for myself occupation-wise, since med school was certainly not in the cards. The only other options for a "good Jewish boy," or so I thought at the time, were basically limited to law school or finance. I never understood how people could simply flock to law school in herds without even a glimmer of an idea of what they stand for. As far as I was concerned, the majority of law students didn't have a clue why they were aside from the promise of a potential six-figure salary and a pat on the back from their parents or rabbi. On top of that, corporate America epitomized the cookie-cutter herd mentality that I have always opposed. I truly had a lot to work out, but for the time being, my focus happily converged upon one thought: seeing Molly.

* * *

Immigration was painless and I had no problem withdrawing one thousand korunas. One yuan was valued at approximately 2.75 korunas. My forty-minute taxi into Praha cost me about five hundred korunas, or twenty-five dollars, give or take. As I was driven through the rural inbetweenness of the airport and the city, I was rather absorbed in the density of Prague. Its coloring reminded me of the dusty pastel chalk that little kids scribble on elementary school playgrounds, only there was clearly nothing playful about it. The city carried a thick emotional undertone, possibly because of the Velvet Revolution and recent turnover from communism to capitalism.

I arrived at the hotel address she gave me and found that she had left me a key at the front desk. The room was pure chaos, with the clothing and bags of at least four people. Molly walked in and she looked like I felt; her mind scrambled, at a complete loss for words. I said hi to her and we embraced. We had sex, but it was detached, like our own sense of our selves at the time. Afterward, my mind was racing, and I could see hers was as well, but not at the same frequency or wavelength. There was a lot of noise in our connection. I was disconcerted and absent-minded by the time we left the hotel to explore.

Molly kept asking me the next day as we walked through the city, "How do you like my Little Praha?" It really was where she belonged, at least for a period. Prague is like a living fairy tale with a castle on top of a hill overlooking the city and enough shades of pink and purple to make any imaginative girl crown herself princess of the land. We walked all day with no destination in mind as we absorbed the majesty of one of the few preserved cities spared during World War II. She would attend class until early afternoon while I roamed around with my new digital camera that I had purchased impulsively in Shanghai and took some beautiful shots of the city until Molly and I met up later. We ended up fighting intermittently as we tried to get used to being around each other again. It was a slow and turbulent reconciliation. I could sense we were moving on from each other. It was a sad but liberating notion.

We had dinner the next night with a couple of her friends at an Italian restaurant near the center of town and found ourselves at a somewhat rundown bar for the remainder of the night. To my surprise there was a bottle of absinthe, the legendary hallucinogenic alcohol banned in the US. I took shots with two of Molly's buddies from the program, one of whom I was sure had a crush on her. It tasted like a mixture of Cool Mint Listerine combined with liquefied black licorice and moonshine. It was harsh, but it still went down better than some tequila. Later, in the great Eastern European moonlight, I was chasing the green fairy until exhaustion.

By my third day in Prague, I realized that something had to be done about my little Chinese visa problem. I took a taxi to the Chinese Embassy and found my way in through a back entrance. There was a cranky Czech woman tending the front desk while the rest of the department took the week off in honor of the Moon Festival. She informed me that if I had tried yesterday they would have been able to accommodate me, but there was nothing that could be done for me at this point. I chuckled to myself and left.

By the last full day together, we had found our groove. It felt like old times in New Orleans. I don't know how it happened, but finally our energies synergized and we could enjoy each other, finally. Whether it was a last-minute mimicry of our former selves, or if we did truly fall back into it for one last moment, I'm not sure. It was too late, though.

As I stood in line at the airport in Prague, it was very difficult for Molly and me to say goodbye. We had always been better together than apart, and even though it took a little while for us to get back in the rhythm, by the end of my trip we were living a dream. Now it was time to wake up. She asked me to stay with her, but I knew that was not an option for me. She mentioned that a lot of poets got their start and lived good lives in Prague. I didn't see how that was relevant to me, and we said our goodbyes.

I took off for Paris and from Paris to Shanghai. I sat next to a wealthy-looking Arab individual about my age en route to Shanghai. He was one of those Europeanized Arabs with his Diesel sneakers and artsy, metrosexual attire. We exchanged a few words and both ended up sleeping most of the way back. As we stood in the two-hour-long bloated catastrophe of an immigration line, I somehow ended up a good twenty people in front of him. At a few feet from the passport checkpoint, I nodded at him as they called my name and subsequently forfeited my travel documents to the female immigration officer in a nonchalant fashion. She eyed my passport with robotic precision and called my bluff within seconds. Unfazed, I figured I would pay a fine and the situation would resolve itself. She called upon an armed security officer and I was ushered down a white hallway into a back room. The whole scenario spawned an image of an American soldier in Vietnam being whisked away by his communist captors for an unfortunate torture session. While I knew this was not actually the case, the severity of the officer's reaction probably should have put me at some degree of uneasiness, but instead I couldn't be more amused. It was situations like these that made me feel alive, similar to the way I felt after I had jumped out of a plane with Jay and a couple of other guys from my fraternity a few years back, or on the many instances where Molly and I would crash our skulls together at full force as a ringing reminder to our brains that we exist.

I was having the time of my life as the Chinese officer informed me that I was going to be deported. Ahmad had called me at that very moment and asked me when I was coming back to the Xinyu Hotel so we could hit the bars. I gave him the low down. Basically my options were to fly back to Paris and allow Air France to incur the eight-hundred-dollar penalty in addition to the cost of my return airfare for failing to check my visa prior to my departure for Shanghai, or I could fly to Hong Kong and pay the penalty myself. Ahmad advised that I fly to Hong Kong and take care of business there and I concurrently agreed. While I did consider flying back to Paris and eventually to Prague to take Molly up on her offer to stay with her for the rest of her fall semester abroad, I knew I would ultimately be shortchanging myself with such a course of action. I handed over my credit card; I was racking up quite a bill.

I woke up early in the bed of my airport hotel in order to make sure my one full day in the city of Hong Kong did not go to waste. I walked through the hotel lobby and down a connecting escalator to the airport's main floor. I quickly honed in on the desk in charge of issuing visas to mainland China. Hong Kong is actually a subtropical island located on the southeastern shore of the mother country. While the British did cede its governmental rights to the once imperially ruled Hong Kong at the turn of the century, from an economic standpoint, Hong Kong is considered a sovereign territory. Fortunately for me, an American passport would suffice upon entrance to Hong Kong. The individuals at the desk were very helpful as they informed me my re-entrance visa would be available the following morning and even recommended a hotel I could stay in for less than half of what I paid the night before. I exchanged my korunas for Hong Kong dollars, which are nearly equivalent in value to the yuan, and caught the next monorail for a forty-minute Disney-esque ride into the heart of Hong Kong. I then took a complimentary bus to a simple hotel whose Chinese name escapes me.

I threw my bag full of what was not entirely dirty laundry into my room and walked outside with the map of the city that I had received upon check-in. Hong Kong was clearly very different from Shanghai, I remember observing. While they are both somewhat dirty, there is a level of sophistication present in Hong Kong that one would expect to find in a city whose identity has already been established. There is no denying the grandeur that is Shanghai, but it is a young city in its overly exuberant adolescence. There is also an undeniable British influence in Hong Kong, visible in its traffic patterns driven by cars equipped with steering wheels on the right side and the architecture of some of the fancier five-star hotels I walked past: more stately and classically old-fashioned than the energetic decadence one would find in Shanghai. There was no mistaking that I was still in China, however; there was no shortage of annoying street salesman trying to peddle their latest pirated copy of *Sin City* on DVD or a brand-new two-cent Rolex.

After a couple of hours of exploring, I ended up at the waterfront gazing at all the fishing boats streaming through the river at a sea turtle–like pace. Hong Kong certainly was not in any rush, rather like Shanghai, I remember half-thinking as I parachuted down from Bri Bri Land.

I decided I would return to the waterfront at night. I knew from the map I had scanned briefly that the Hong Kong Science Museum with an IMAX theatre was not far away. I have been to my share of science museums back in the States and figured it would be interesting to see the Chinese version. I am always interested to see how different frames of thought approach the same subject, especially when this matter is something as theoretically objective and universal as science. Science is not supposed to be like art, where meaning and purpose are largely a function of interpretation, though it is my perception that even science has somewhat of a gray area and is subject to a degree of interpretive bias.

I purchased a ticket to the IMAX theatre's tribute to Albert Einstein and the theory of relativity. I sat and watched with a gigantic headset similar to the one I used to drown out the world at college. I listened in English. It turned out to be a strange phenomenon, since I could hear the Chinese through the earphones just as easily as I could hear the English emanating from the speakers suctioned to my ears. I pondered the visual image of Einstein riding a lightning bolt into space as part of a humorous demonstration of the minimal effect of time in relation to an object traveling at the speed of light. That image was possibly being interpreted in profoundly different ways, depending on which language the audience heard. *Is* science the one common platform of thought where the Eastern and Western worlds are on the exact same page? It is a gray area, in my opinion.

I returned to the waterfront and stared at the glowing Hong Kong skyline before I headed back to the hotel and left for Shanghai the next morning, this time with a proper visa. I emailed Jamie from the business center at the airport hotel to notify him about the likely possibility of missing a couple of days of work due to my unexpected detour. He didn't make a big deal about it when I returned, but the rest of Vision Asia was astounded by my deportation story. Ironically, most of the people I worked with had never in their entire lives as Chinese citizens ever seen Hong Kong, and here I was, a tourist in their eyes, educating them about one of their own cities. Belinda told me it was nice to have "Mel Gibson" back in the office to keep her company. Maybe it was the wavy hair, or the American features, but something about being compared to the likes of Mel Gibson did not exactly appeal to me, as much as I doubt he would care to be measured against a Jew, unless that Jew was Jesus. No offense to Jesus. As a characterization of a young American adult in a foreign land without a meaningful understanding of American pop culture, I suppose Mel Gibson will do, much like Jackie Chan for lack of a better way to stereotype all the Asians I went to high school with.

October 31 was my last day working at Vision Asia. The focus of my remaining month and a half in Shanghai adjusted itself to partying and traveling, two crucial components of any recent college graduate's complete abroad experience. Ahmad and I met some very interesting characters during this period. We found ourselves rendezvousing at a lounge named Barbarossa situated exotically in the middle of a man-made lake in People's Square Park. It was a bastion of capitalistic decadence and aesthetics juxtaposed in the center of a communist square. A short bridge guided us across the moat and into the royal Moroccan-themed tent, where the heavy exhalation of smoke from the hookah tent caressed the gentle nighttime air with a tender and glowing defiance before it in its gradual and winding diffusion was lost to the human eye. Jonah, the bartender, a former Miami native, would mix us a couple of strong blueberry mojitos, a new twist on an old Cuban favorite, on the house of course. Ahmad worked methodically like Oscar Schindler, exerting his impressive talent for schmoozing and meeting new people that led us to all the perks inherent in being on a first-name basis with many of the city's club managers and bartenders. I was more laid back and not nearly as socially motivated in Shanghai, though I certainly appreciated Ahmad's abilities.

We met "the Italian guys," Antonio and Armeno, during a late night at Bar Rouge, where Moët & Chandon was the theme of the night. The Italian guys were a couple of fashionable playboys with their white sport coats and their designer Armani jeans. Coming from the US, I was not used to seeing heterosexual men so obsessed with style (outside of New York City, at least), though eventually I came to realize that this is fairly typical of European males, especially those from Italy. Between the two, Armeno was the only Italian guy who could manage fluent English, having spent a couple of years in his early childhood living in Chicago with his Native American uncle. He would proudly suggest that he was more American than I am, which in a way I guess is true, though he and Antonio both proudly represented Naples. I couldn't manage to decipher exactly what their business in Shanghai revolved around. Something to do with importing and exporting mini-bike engines. It was all the same to me, anyway, as they made an exciting and eclectic addition to our melting pot of international acquaintances.

Hanna, a German skydiver and ambitious young businesswoman with a thing for Chinese men (and women) was part of the Abroad China program as well, and began to roll around with us to all the late-night spots. Vision Asia was but a faded impression in my mind as I began to drown myself in the excesses of the party scene once again. I drank because it made me feel the freedom of a lawless inner world of imagination and soul, a world I always willed for myself beyond the structure of parental and Jewish cultural expectations. My heart would thump to the beat of the Shanghai house music as the thugged-out Westernized Chinese would flow into the clubs like mindless wannabe gangster drones struggling with the ancient traditions and the promises of the future. Chrome-plated earpieces rested decadently on the sides of their skulls to match their miniaturized three-hundred-dollar cell phones in one hand, a cup of green tea with a dash of Jack Daniels whiskey to complement the other.

In New Orleans, we used to frequent a bar on the outskirts of a New Orleans ghetto called Butler's, a rundown shack complete with beefed-up security guards, the best in gangster rap deejays, an old-school Atari in the corner, and the most fascinating collection of Tulane students and African Americans from the streets. The integrated crowd had a distant harmony to it—until a couple of people got murdered and the bar closed. The Shanghai club scene in no way matched the intensity of the bar that was once Butler's no matter how hard the Chinese tried to mimic the hip-hop culture of the West. It was a dilute replica at best, a manufactured simulacrum.

Eventually, Ahmad and I decided it was time to take a trip outside Shanghai, as his hot little Serbian girlfriend had become the source of more emotional annoyance than he was willing to deal with, and similarly, Molly and I were in the midst of our own relationship woes as we began fighting over the phone every time we spoke. It had been a solid month since she asked me to stay with her in Prague, and a lot had changed; neither of us had ever handled being apart with any type of emotional maturity. Thailand was the destination, a mere four hours or so away from the Shanghai Pudong Airport. We were all set to purchase tickets until Ahmad remembered to check the Thai embassy website and see if his Lebanese passport would be enough to get him across the border, which inevitably it was not, as Thailand is as one of the many countries whose entrance requirements are stricter in regards to Middle Eastern documentation. Ahmad would have had to apply for a visa months in advance, even though a US passport holder could pass through with ease. Considering my own recent experience with the Chinese immigration line, neither of us were willing to take a chance in Thailand and decided on the island of Hainan, home of the famous beach town of Sanya—our destination.

＊

We arrived at night after a two-hour flight and immediately delighted in the instantly recognizable island breeze. We took a taxi to Resort Horizon, situated beautifully atop the smooth ambiance of the Yalong Bay. The next morning, we woke up and realized that aside from a Russian couple we had met the first night at the bar, Resort Horizon's vacationers were as homogeneously Chinese as Beijing's diplomatic cabinet. Gone was the mix of Americans and Europeans we were accustomed to in the metropolis of Shanghai. We realized quickly that we were in China's version of Florida, where the land of China comes to warm up and be a kid.

Ahmad and I were sitting on the beach after an hour of dodging little light bulb–shaped jellyfish during our hour of snorkeling, observing in astonishment as the vacationing Chinese men and women chased each other around the sand, all wearing the same blue hotel robe, in a game of what looked to us to be no more complex than tag. They were like little children laughing and giggling as I postulated to Ahmad that only a country with a one-child policy could produce such a childlike, self-indulgent attitude. Meanwhile, I was completely lost in another world, just stalling until real-life decisions needed to be made. I was off the Adderall and on a lot of other stuff.

Our time at Resort Horizon and the first couple of days in Sanya were more than enjoyable. By the third day, we decided to venture over to the Sheraton a few hotels down the beach to eat lunch and hopefully discover a finer crop of young ladies than what we found at the Resort Horizon. To our immediate surprise, within the first couple of minutes on the Sheraton property, we passed by some of the most beautiful women we had ever seen anywhere, let alone in China, let alone on the island of Hainan, the unexpected last place on the planet that either Ahmad or myself would ever have dreamt to be the home of the Miss World Pageant 2005. With a familiar sped-up impulsiveness that felt routine, I reserved the rest of our stay at the Sheraton Hotel, which I rationalized was pennies a night cheaper and more attractive. Another swipe of the credit card.

The second day at the Sheraton, Ahmad received a call in our room from Miss Botswana's mother, who was very worried about her daughter and had tried vehemently, with a thick African accent, to reason with the Mandarin-speaking front desk attendant to connect her to her daughter's room, the room of Miss Botswana. The best the front desk could manage was our room—quite the arbitrary choice, but nevertheless a blessing in disguise. Ahmad assured Miss Botswana's mother that we would find her daughter and have her call immediately. Ahmad and I immediately went downstairs and snuck past the prowling chaperones and over to a young beauty who turned out to be Miss France. We excused ourselves and asked her to please direct us to Miss Botswana, as we had an urgent message from her mother. Miss France took this in good humor and pointed across the hall to Miss Nigeria, and behind her, Miss Botswana. Miss Botswana thanked us both with a sincere smile and whispered to me that Miss Nigeria had a crush on me. I laughed, wondering if it was true. It had to be; I told them to meet us later on at the bar and lounge in the lobby and to bring a handful of their friends. They agreed but never actually showed. I blame the chaperones.

I ended up spending the night with the pretty twenty-year-old Paraguayan vocalist who serenaded the hotel guests with a group of guitarists. I just kept telling her, *Me gusta sus ojas* ("I like your eyes"). Her voice was sweet and her hair was like a flowing stream of dark chocolate. We slept together and she spent the remaining hours of the night peeling the burnt layers of skin off my back and repeatedly called me *serpiente* as she applied more lotion to my raw, exposed skin. Ahmad still jokes that somewhere in China is a spunky Paraguayan boy with a Jewish nose and ADHD looking for his father. (I'm right here!)

A week later, I was wandering aimlessly around Beijing with no sense of past or future.

Chapter 8
Homeless in Beijing

I purchased a roundtrip train ticket to Beijing soon after Ahmad left for Miami. (Ahmad had family in Miami despite not being a citizen at the time.) There was something about traveling to Beijing alone that appealed to me, and I did exactly that; I needed to be alone. Shanghai's train station was only two subway stops away from the Xinyu Hotel, and it was not too difficult to navigate my way through the mass of Chinese travelers and board my train. The ticket cost me fifty American dollars, easily enough currency to feed a Chinese family of four for a week and a half. I was the first of four members in my sleeper cabin to arrive. One by one, Shanghai's upper crust took claim to their cot. The last to enter was a young man whose Tai Chi–like climbing ability led him gracefully over my neighbor's bed and onto the top bunk with the grace of a ballerina. The atmosphere was friendly and non-committal, as we all shared a mutual respect for each other's space without any additional desire to engage in even the most superficial conversation. The young lady next to me was dressed to compete among Shanghai's highest in societal stature. Sometime before I dozed off, I recall having trouble dealing with whatever monstrosity of a fruit they decided to serve us alongside our shredded pork and white rice. She robotically explained that the fruit is normally referred to as *lychee*, or the "dragon's eye." After peeling off the sharp outer membrane, there was a lusciously moist inner fruit the size of a ping pong ball that was quite sweet and tasty.

I fell asleep with ease as my body adjusted itself in anticipation of a long trip. I woke up intermittently to see the lights of identical-looking factory towns. The lights in our cabin turned on not long after the sun began to illuminate the sliding landscape outside my window. As we approached Beijing, I remember seeing a handful of Chinese men and women in their backyards performing their morning Tai Chi sessions. I figure Tai Chi serves as a much healthier attempt at stimulating the senses in the morning than the Adderall pop Americans depend on. As we pulled into the station, I felt a jolt of excitement, the kind that normally hits me when I have arrived at an undiscovered territory in my imagination. In preparation for my trip to Beijing, all I had was a couple of days' worth of clean clothes and the address of the Holiday Inn.

It was early morning sometime in early December as the soles of my Nike Airs made contact with the freezing cement of the train station. I knew I had to act fast to find a taxi before the intolerable wind chill iced over my steady stride. Latitude-wise, Beijing resides about parallel with the southernmost portion of Mongolia, which is nestled right below Russia.

Within minutes after emerging to the street, I began to move in slow motion due to the cold. I crossed to the other side of the street opposite the train station and hailed a cab about ten minutes later. With the best translation I could manage, I spoke the name of the street of the Beijing Holiday Inn. The driver had no idea of the hotel's whereabouts and passed me on to another who knew of the street I was searching for. The hotel was just off a main highway running through the city and boasted a festively decorated marble-floored lobby with an overexcited Christmas theme to make all the Western travelers feel at home. I approached the counter and spoke my name to the female clerk. She greeted me warmly and asked to see my passport. This question struck me as ludicrous. I explained to her that I traveled by train from Shanghai and that no passport was necessary. She told me that all international travelers must show their passports when checking into a hotel in the People's Republic of China. I subsequently assured her that I clearly was

not an international traveler because I HAD ARRIVED FROM
SHANGHAI; I was, therefore, a domestic traveler. At that point
I was sure of two things: I was right and I was not going to win
this battle.

The hotel clerk, whose initial smile had morphed into an
expressionless clinical void representative of the systematic red
tape she was now guardian of, told me coldly, "We cannot let
you into hotel without WISA."

I said, "Do you mean, *visa*?"

She said, "Yes, no entry without WISA."

I walked away from the counter with the realization that my
trip to Beijing would have to be a very short one unless I wanted
to risk freezing to death on the streets. I walked for miles down
the superhighway that ran perpendicular to the hotel street,
looking for a crosswalk. I wanted to get across the street to a
China Construction Bank, one of the banks I knew would accept
my ATM card. I thought, *Why in the world is there not even
one opportunity to cross the street?* In New Jersey, the highway
capital of the world, and the state where I spent the majority of
my twenty-three years, cement highway divides have a gap in
them approximately every half-mile to allow for U-turns. These
same gaps provide brave pedestrians the opportunity to cross
over. I had never seen a highway with no gap until the day it was
imperative that I cross the street in the city of Beijing.

I hailed a cab and told him to take me across the street.
He laughed and told me in indecipherable Chinese, "Get out."
Finally, I decided I would have to climb over the divide. I made
it through traffic and to the other side with little conflict. From
an aerial vantage point, I must have looked like Frogger, moving
erratically in an effort to dodge an ever-flowing stream of traffic.
I believe this very concept is addressed in a *Seinfeld* episode
where George has to carry an arcade-sized video game machine
across the street while maneuvering his way through oncoming
traffic.

I was able to withdraw enough cash to pay for the seven-
hundred-yuan fare I would incur after a day with a rouge taxi
driver. When I made it back to the Holiday Inn, my driver was
waiting in his early nineties Volkswagen Jetta, similar to the taxis
in Shanghai, except this one was jet black. I told the man at the

door of the hotel that brokered our arrangement that I wanted to see the Great Wall of China followed by the Forbidden City.

The Great Wall materialized within my consciousness about an hour outside the city of Beijing. At first glance, before I began to scale the immensely tiring set of stairs, I felt a moment of déjà vu. Just like in Shanghai and the rest of China, there were enough Chinese salesmen with their inane little gadgets, decorative tidbits, and homemade garments to entertain and clothe an island full of hyperactive toddlers. This time I bit, though. It was imperative, before I climbed another couple hundred feet, that I pay homage to my frostbitten fingers and numb skull with some mittens and a puffy red woven snow cap. Later, when I communicated to my driver by raising two fingers on my right hand to indicate that I had paid two American dollars for both items, he told me I got ripped off.

I climbed the last of what seemed like an endless series of stone block steps, each of which were chiseled out to be about a foot in height each. My lungs were so frigid I could feel them hardening, and my organs were slowing down. There were periodic fortifications within the Wall and these contained even more salesmen with more garments and more gizmos. My mind flashed back to an image of men and women in American shopping malls with their mobile carts and personalized T-shirts and caps trying to make a buck. Funny how some concepts are so universal that your mind can make instantaneous connections to things worlds away faster than any of Intel's most powerful processors. It is a certainty that human life is rapidly becoming more dependent upon machines as the economy continues to globalize. But there is one thing a machine will never master in the foreseeable future—abstract thinking. The day a computer develops the ability to think abstractly is the day machines are no longer confined to the actions for which they are programmed. It is also the day we run for our lives.

Prophecy aside, I have always had a real interest in the duality of the mind and the brain and what constitutes consciousness.

I reached the pinnacle of my trip to the top step of the uppermost fortification, a tower above me. I looked out in sheer amazement at the Great Wall of China snaking its way over, around, and in between the hills beyond the horizon of my perception. I thought at that very moment that all of this trekking was going to be worth it in the long run, even though I had another hour's ride back into the heart of Beijing to feast my eyes on the Forbidden City. I hadn't given any thought as to how I was going to survive the night without a hotel room. In any case, I took one last look at the grandeur of the Great Wall of China and climbed back down the stairs and back through the parking lot with the salesmen, tapped the window of the black Jetta to wake my trusty napping driver, and we were off.

I dozed off for a bit as we drove back toward the city, though I did notice the sign on the highway to turn off for the Ming Tombs, the burial grounds of an ancient Chinese emperor. The mountainous vista gave way to a sprawling urban center with a crowd of little shops and Chinese men huddling around the warmth of their woks and steamers.

I was dropped off about a mile outside the entrance to the Forbidden City. I traced the perimeter of the gigantic walls surrounding it. The Forbidden City, from what I understand about ancient Chinese history, is a city within a city. The city outside the Forbidden City was poor and depressed, while the city inside the walls represented all that was rich and decadent among the governing class, and especially the emperor himself. The peasants eventually became fed up with the aberrant inequalities, and the emperor was overthrown. In my eyes, it is another testament to the dangers inherent in complacency and the failure to acknowledge those who are hungry and compete for food, money, intellectual progression, scientific innovation, or the very job one currently occupies.

The Forbidden City itself looked like an expansive village rather than a city, per se. It is quite a sight no matter how you look at it, though. Chinese tourists lined up from all over the land of China to breathe in the ancient aroma of a bygone civilization. You have seen the Forbidden City in movies, whether you realize it or not. A few hundred feet separates the entrance and the emperor's house, used for political gatherings and diplomatic rendezvous. As I navigated my way through the various houses and art galleries, it became more real to me. I found myself in the emperor's garden and took a quick glance into a multitude of houses built solely for the emperor's mistresses. Funny as it is to think about—or tragic, really—each mistress was brought up to serve the king through years of training as part of a hierarchal institution. In other words, there were different ranks or levels of mistress a female could occupy, much like the various tiers to the Great Wall.

The cold had long ago penetrated my brand-new woven red hat and mittens, so I figured it was time to start moving again. I drummed my way through the crowds and ultimately outside the walls of the Forbidden City. I exited from a different point than where I initially arrived so I would be just a short distance from Tiananmen Square. The view of the square from across the street was dreamlike, almost as if I had been there before. I took a stairway underground and surfaced minutes later. The wind shifted from every direction, much like a racquetball ball can blindside you from any angle. The flags in the air flew with greater force and prominence than the one that would sometimes send me into a trance on top of Bar Rouge overlooking Pudong. After all, I was in the capital of Beijing, or Peking, to the natives. It was a short—even eerie—stay for me in Tiananmen. I could feel the suffering of the thousands of students and Red Cross workers who died in the 1989 massacre.

Consistent with a long tradition of the Chinese government's unwillingness to acknowledge their own actions under the guise of censorship, a Chinese resident can find him or herself in a heap of trouble by mentioning the massacre in front of the wrong government official. Chinese tourists must keep their mouths shut as they gaze at one of Beijing's greatest attractions. Tiananmen Square carried an odd, medicinal feeling to it, almost like the strange sensation one feels when breathing in the newly applied bleach meant to cover the mess of a blood-soaked hospital emergency room.

After my self-guided tour of Tiananmen, I retraced my steps back around the walls of the Forbidden City and over to the parking lot that my driver was waiting in. He dropped me back off at "my hotel," where he told me the price of his services would be eight hundred yuan, or about ninety dollars. Granted, I was tired, but I remembered distinctly that our negotiation called for seven hundred yuan—not eight hundred. I chuckled at his foiled attempt and enjoyed a quick lunch at the hotel buffet before I flagged another taxi and handed him the card with the Chinese characters meant to indicate "train station."

* * *

The sun was setting as I finished the solid seven or eight hours of my one-day tour of China's capital city. While I would have liked to stay longer, I did the best I could to condense my experience into the raw essentials of any Westerner's touring expectations, and I felt I did a fairly good job in light of the circumstances. I approached the ticketing window expecting to trade my one-way ticket back, dated three days from that very moment, for a pass for that night. Unfortunately, all the sleeper tickets were sold out and the only remaining vacancies were standing room only, a concept unheard of in the US. I had two choices: Stand shoulder to shoulder with other Chinese travelers looking for the cheapest possible way to get to Shanghai in eleven hours on an overnight train, or wander the streets of Beijing homeless, which in a sense I was already, and wait the three days out for my sleeper train.

I sat there for hours in the dark trying to figure out a another way, and just as I was about to hand my money over to the attendant and purchase one standing-room-only ticket for what was roughly ten dollars, I received an enthusiastic tap on the shoulder from an unidentified Chinese man. He was searching for recruits to fill his bus that was leaving for Shanghai within the hour. At first, I was a bit hesitant about the proposition, but considering the alternative, I had to at least entertain the idea. He led me over to his bus filled with eager Chinese travelers tucked neatly into their bobsled-sized personal sleepers. I handed the owner thirty yuan, which ended up being cheaper than purchasing an entirely new sleeper pass on the train. Granted, I would have stood the entire duration of the trip had I gone with the cheapest option, but this, to me, seemed even more adventurous, as I had a hard time even imagining a stretch of highway spanning the overwhelming distance between Beijing to Shanghai—more than one thousand kilometers, to be more succinct. I boarded the bus and walked slowly toward the middle of the aisle before I threw my bag inside the basket at the end of the sleeper I would claim as my own on the top row. I jammed my feet inside the partially enclosed end of the "bed" and chuckled at the scenario at hand. Picture yourself climbing inside a bobsled near the ceiling of the bus for the night with nothing but what seems to be raw cotton to keep you warm.

As the bus departed, one of the passengers approached me with a mischievous smile and greeted me foolishly: "HELLO." This was followed by a rapid succession of hellos from everyone on the bus. The whole bus was cracking up. Better than murderous stares, I thought to myself as laughed with them.

I was the only English-speaking passenger on a bus of twenty or so Chinese, making me feel as if I was in a Kung Fu movie like the one that was playing. Often, when I watch a movie, my mind will tune out or fail to process dialogue. Shortly after the first movie was finished, we stopped off on the highway about two hours outside Beijing and enjoyed a buffet full of what I think— and very much hoped—was beef alongside a never-ending community bowl of white rice and other random complements that escape my memory. I don't think some of the people in the restaurant had ever seen a white man, as I received some astonished glances.

I did my best to clamp down on my rice and beef specialty with my chopsticks. There are certain aspects of etiquette that would catch a Westerner off-guard in China. From what I have seen, a Chinese individual will not hesitate to stare at you if something captivates them. In the States, it is, of course, rude to stare, no matter how badly your eyes would like to lock onto the object or person of interest for just a few seconds longer. My friend and former co-worker, Tiffany, who, as mentioned previously, is about six feet and blond, used to draw the most blatantly prolonged stares. While more Westerners are flocking to China as I write this, it is important to keep in mind that China is larger than the continental US, and there are still areas where the Chinese have not ever seen a white person.

As the bus moved on, I found myself dozing off midway into the second martial arts movie and ended up staying asleep for a solid four hours or so. When I woke up, the bus was pitch-black and silent. The only sounds were the whisk of the road flying by and the subtle sound of a man snoring in the back. The highway was dimly lit and I wondered for a second whether I was ever actually going to be back in Shanghai. I lay awake for the next couple of hours in contemplation of my trip to Beijing and the somewhat ludicrous materialization of events. I fell asleep for a second time only to be awakened by the bus driver himself at around seven in the morning telling me that I had to get off and transfer to the next bus, which happened to be parked parallel to our position. On top of his directions I could hear a chorus of "Hello . . . Hello . . . Hello . . ." behind me as if to sing me off the premises.

I smiled as I laced up my Nike Air Maxes and boarded the next bus. It was an ordinary blue bus like the last one, except it boasted actual seats rather than little shelf-like sleepers. I looked out the window for the next two hours as the landscape began to transition into the familiar light greenish-brown marshland of outer Shanghai. We passed through Suzhou, a suburb of Shanghai, oriented toward mostly rice fields, irrigation, and the occasional water buffalo. We made a couple of more stops before we finally ended at the Shanghai bus station near the outskirts of the French Concession with about a fifteen-minute taxi to the Xinyu Hotel.

* * *

By the time I returned from Beijing, it was nearing the end of the year. I remained in Shanghai for about two weeks more. Ahmad was already in Miami and I wondered when, if ever, I would see him again. I spent my remaining days reading a lot and occasionally going out with the Italian guys; Hanna and even Angela tagged along on occasion.

While I could probably write an entire book on my experiences in China alone, I figure it is time to move on. I was back in Holmdel by the new year for what proved to be a painfully depressing wake-up call. It was time to figure out what was next, and fast. I had convinced myself, or at least partially convinced myself, that the right thing to do, coming back from Shanghai with no intention to go to law school or medical school, was to go into finance. That would still make the family proud and allow me the chance to make a living. It seemed to me that I was going to have to make a few adjustments, at least on the surface, to my once-negative point of view toward the business world and especially corporate America. I knew philosophy was not going to pay the bills, and I had my chance at medicine and failed. My conversations with Molly were becoming more infrequent with passing time and that saddened me as I knew we were slipping away from each other. I was going to have to suck this one up and get a job and put the past behind me, despite the impossibility of that very notion.

Chapter 9
Morgan Stanley

Despite all I had gone through and the global expansion of my perspective on life, I was sucked back to New Jersey for the beginning of 2006 only to try and convince Morgan Stanley to hire a philosophy major fresh off the slow boat from China to sell mutual funds and alternative investments. It was going to be my last attempt at fitting the blue print. The pressure I was putting on myself all of the sudden was boiling up in my chest. I knew the time to get a job, for the sake of my own sanity, would have to come sooner than later. Most of my friends were still in New Orleans, Miami, Shanghai—anywhere besides Holmdel.

During my weeks spent laying on the couch watching TV like a deadbeat lump of inanimate matter, I communicated with my cousin Scott, an employee of the Merrill Lynch Investment Management Division, to prep myself for the various questions I would be confronted with as I interviewed for various entry-level financial positions. Both my cousins, Steve and Scott, have always treated me more like a little brother than a cousin and I have tremendous gratitude for all the things they have shown me over the years. When Scott heard that I was interested in finance, he did everything he could to prepare me. We went over voice projection, basic financial knowledge, potential interview questions, and most importantly, my mess of a résumé.

A résumé seemed unnecessary. Cleary one could not judge one's character or intelligence by their grade point average and summer internships. Scott told me about the giant stack of recommendations he had collected during his time in college and said I should think about emailing a couple of my professors for their endorsements. I figured this, too, was unnecessary, as I figured my own recommendation of myself upon interviewing would suffice. I had never bothered to get to know any of my professors in college and did not feel right asking them for a recommendation, despite the fact that I was sure they would not have a problem with any request of mine. It felt artificial.

There was one exception. Second semester senior year I had the same professor for my 200-level modern philosophy class and my 600-level graduate philosophy class, Empiricism. Oliver Sensen had earned his PhD at Cambridge and spent a few years teaching at Harvard before electing to take a professorship at Tulane University. After he administered the second quiz of the semester, he approached me after class and asked me why I was not performing at the high level on quizzes that he had come to expect at that point given the quality of my comments in class. He went on to tell me that I had a lot of potential and he did not understand why my grades were not reflecting such. Almost four years at Tulane and this was the first I had ever heard such a thing from a teacher. I told him later that I did not mean to insult him by failing to live up to my potential and that maybe my ADHD had something to do with my underperformance. It was the first time I had ever used it as a scapegoat, but I did not want him to lose his confidence in me, or re-think his comments from earlier in the semester. I could tell he really did believe that ADHD could impede academic performance. Looking back, I am sure he would have been curious to know most of the auditory components of his lecture never made it beyond the semi-permeable membrane between the outside world and my brain.

In any case, I did stop by and speak with him once after class. I cannot recall what the meeting was about, but it was monumental in the sense that I voluntarily chose to meet with one of my professors beyond the classroom setting. I think we discussed New Orleans college students' boozing habits, but

I couldn't say for sure. Later, when Katrina hit, which I only dodged by two weeks, I sent him an email to see if he and his family were okay. Molly accused me sucking up to get a letter of recommendation from him and I even admitted, falsely, that maybe it was the reason. It wasn't, though; I genuinely cared that he made it out because to me there was no more valuable a professor on the Tulane campus than Oliver Sensen. I never asked him for a recommendation and resented the idea of asking any teacher.

* * *

Scott looked at one of the last of my countless redrafts and told me everything was spotless, except that I would have a hard time convincing any employer that I was a professional snowboarder, as I boldly pointed out on my résumé at the bottom under "activities." While I was a professional in my own mind, he assured me that I would need to be sponsored or at least have a few medals in my possession to back my claim. I assured my cousin I would remove that element before any distributions were in order, but that I really was "awesome" at snowboarding.

My first interview was at Smith Barney for the financial consulting trainee program. Essentially, this was a fancy name for a stock broker trainee program. I made it through the first interview and was invited back for a second. Luckily, a family friend, a gracious man by the name of Mark Smith, was a financial advisor for the company I really wanted to work for, Morgan Stanley, and he was marvelous in his endeavor to secure me an interview with Morgan Stanley Investment Management. A job with MS Investment Management held a few key points of significance for me. For one, I would not have to interrupt families during dinner with the latest in securities offerings (though looking back, it wouldn't have been so bad), and two, I would be able to work with mutual funds, which I felt would be a good segue into the hedge fund industry in due time.

I went through the first stage of interviewing with a lovely young woman by the name of Jennifer Wolfe. My brain was working well and I answered all the questions with ease, despite the fact that I showed up on the wrong date and time. Jennifer was in contact with the team at the Harbor Side Financial Center in Jersey City to schedule the next round of interviews. Carlo Aprea, vice president and desk manager of the internal sales consultants, greeted me warmly as I emerged from the elevator and onto the third floor of Plaza 2. He escorted me to the room where I was to interview and ultimately present a sales pitch on the topic of my choosing.

We sat face to face, and Carlo asked me in an amused manner, "So, professional snowboarder, huh?"

I belted out a chain of curses a mile long inside my head while outwardly maintaining my composure with a slight chuckle, while politely informing him that he must have been given an outdated resume. I reached inside my black leather folder and handed him my most recent copy since Scott's latest array of constructive criticism. Imagine my relief when Carlo transitioned into his own miniature monologue as he told me about the new Burton snowboard he had just received for Christmas and the house he rents with a few of his friends in Vermont. It's funny how things tend to work out favorably based on some of the most random of circumstances. It was at that moment that I silently thanked Mrs. C., my old Hebrew tutor, for convincing me to use snowboarding as my topic of choice for my sales pitch rather than *The Simpsons*, my favorite TV show.

Mrs. C. explained to me a couple of days before my interview that my topic needed to come from the heart and represent something that projects the image of a "go-getter" and a "doer," rather than one who merely sits on the couch and takes pleasure in a television show. I agreed and found that I didn't even need the two index cards of bullet points I had prepared the night before. I pictured myself on the mountain in my usual HD-quality imagination and manufactured in my mind the tranquility of the mountains and the continuity of thought and action I delight in as I surf the snow. My body language was in sync with my thoughts, and my speech, which has the tendency to stall itself on occasion like a motorboat running on fumes, was just as fluid. It's truly wondrous how easily I could execute a simple sales pitch on why I enjoy snowboarding and why others might like it as well. When spoken from the heart, words have a magical way of being there when you need them.

The remainder of the interview following my presentation went extremely well as the two members of the team Carlo chose to sit in on the presentation took a noticeable liking to me. Two agonizingly long weeks later, Jennifer Wolfe called me with an offer of employment from Morgan Stanley to be an internal sales consultant for the mutual fund desk.

* * *

My first day of work was February 6, 2006. I would wake up around 6:15 and take the 7:20 a.m. train into Newark Penn Station, where I could transfer to the Path train into Jersey City. The commute took around an hour. Carlo checked me in the first day since I hadn't received an official ID for entrance. I was introduced to everyone and kept to myself at my seat for the first couple of weeks, taking in the new atmosphere and learning about the products I was to sell as soon as Carlo gave me the okay to "go live" on the phones.

Admittedly, I was anxious well into the first few months at Morgan. Carlo would call me into his oversized cube every other day to check in on my progress and train me. I was clearly uncomfortable with one-on-one conversation and found myself fidgeting as Carlo lectured me on various financial concepts. I found myself staring blankly back at him sometimes as he asked me simple questions, questions whose answer I certainly knew, but the knowledge was of little help to me since I did not know what he was asking me. I was still about ten months away from realizing that I have trouble focusing and that entire conversations can expire without my processing a word of it, at least on a conscious level. I would leave Carlo's cube even more anxious and upset than when I would enter it because I knew Carlo was beginning to wonder about me.

Working in the corporate world forced me to face many things about myself because it is a closed and even somewhat controlled environment, where repetitive behaviors tend to magnify themselves in conjunction with a constant setting. In school, I could always bounce around from place to place, class to class. In China, I was all over the place. In the corporate world, I was forced to sit at the same desk for at least eight hours a day and interact with the same people at the same time under the same conditions, Monday through Friday. I hadn't let anyone this close to me in years. Suddenly, I found myself thinking about such things as relationship management. There was no opportunity to hide behind the chaos of my scattered life and flying brain.

They were a good group of individuals, though, and all characters in their own right. I adapted relatively quickly and earned a reputation early on as the type of person to push the limits on things. Rob Mcfarlane and I were notorious as the two rookies who brazenly placed one order each of Johnnie Walker Blue on the company tab at the Havana Club amongst the likes of Al Sharpton and Alec Baldwin in Midtown Manhattan our third and second weeks on the job. Later, when others were talking about what had been done, I overheard someone say, "B-Rob did it," (even though it was Rob who ordered the drinks).

B-Rob caught on again, and over the following couple of months my behavior became increasingly fearless and somewhat outlandish. March was my first month on the phones and I was number one in activity points, which were allotted based upon the number of outbound, inbound, and left messages to financial advisors regarding MS funds. Since training had ended, I was no longer subjected to regular one-on-one lectures from Carlo, and he was able to focus more on my hunger to prove myself on the phones and my more animated way with some of the advisors. I found that if my vision was locked on some sort of object in motion, whether it be a person across the room, a boat floating past my beautiful view of the Hudson River, or a helicopter patrolling the NYC skyline, I was able to pay attention to what was being said to me on the phones with greater clarity and act accordingly. It wasn't perfect, but it helped. As time went on, I began to get more proficient with the products and the industry.

In early May, Carlo dropped a four-inch-thick binder on my desk labeled *Securities Training Corporation*. It was the Series 7 manual. For those not familiar with finance, the Series 7 legally allows an individual to sell securities such as stocks, bonds, mutual funds, funds of hedge funds, and so forth. Each "internal" was given three chances to pass the test, and it just so happened that the employee MS brought me in to replace had been transferred to another department after failing at all three attempts. I knew I could not take any chances. I went home that day and asked my dad for a prescription for a 10 mg Adderall to take in the evening to help me focus.

Ryan Kulik, the newest internal to join since I came on board, was promoted from the customer service desk and had already taken a look at the Series 7 material. We were scheduled to attend classes at the DoubleTree Hotel in Manhattan for the month of May twice a week after work. Inevitably, Ryan began attending class by his lonesome as the class was not doing me any good, as usual. My self-made curriculum would consist of 100 percent self-study with the help of my little blue pills, or vitamin A, as I called them for a bit. At first, one was enough to give me the neuro-stimulative high that my brain would crave in the pursuit of page after page of the laws and regulations put forth by the Securities and Exchange Commission. While there was some good in learning the Series 7 material, the fact was I needed the Adderall to sit me down in one place and study for more than ten minutes at a time. Soon two or three Adderall a day transformed into a mandatory four to get me going on the mundane content that was 85 percent of the Series 7 material. Even with the artificial enhancement, I still found myself zoning out into Bri Bri Land; the only difference was, I had a better time sitting in one spot as my impulsiveness to move around and fidget had been minimized.

I took the Series 7 in early July and passed with an 80 percent. Ryan received an 88 percent. With 70 as the minimum passing grade I was proud of myself, and I was proud of Ryan. I had learned to taper my expectations on tests. I had graduated Tulane University with a meager 2.3 GPA. Adderall was my secret weapon, despite the anti-social effects it had. I figured that if I relegated the drug consumption to an as-needed basis, I could pass any test with night study and still go to work, where I was expected to be at least somewhat social and salesman-like—unmedicated.

By August I had passed the Series 66, which is the combination state law and portfolio management examination. Most internals let at least a year go by before tackling the 66, but with the help of Adderall I was able to pass it with only three weeks of preparation; granted, with a 72 percent, but nevertheless, people were shocked with the two accomplishments spaced together so closely. I found myself meriting more respect in the workplace as my co-workers' perception of me became less that of a punk kid fresh out of college and more of an ambitious young "go-getter." The B-Rob persona was at its peak; I found myself cracking the whole desk up just by acting like myself. Clearly, I had a problem with authority in their eyes, as I would not hesitate to argue my point of view with anyone in upper management.

Unfortunately, the more I learned about the financial services industry, the more I became disillusioned by it. The corporate world was too systematized and political for a free thinker like me to ever truly be happy. I struggled to find meaning in the work I was doing and found very little to work with. I loved the people I was with and that kept me going for a while, but predictably, it was not enough to sustain my spirit. I once again turned to Adderall in September to study for my chartered financial analyst designation. I decided that I would have to get out of sales since I was having increasing trouble being salesman-like, or as I saw it, phony in my endeavor to represent products I wasn't passionate about.

My ACT score dropped off steadily as my relationship with the external wholesaler I was assigned to became strained. Our territory consisted of Southern California, including Los Angeles, in addition to the Las Vegas area in Nevada. Andrew was, in a sense, my boss just as Carlo was, and it was my job to follow up with any advisors he may have met with, and to fulfill various merchandise (favors for clients like T-shirts, pens, and other paraphernalia) orders he would allot to the advisors to encourage them to keep doing business with Morgan Stanley. I would end up receiving these orders and ultimately botching them. On top of that, the various administrative tasks he would ask me to do would often remain unfinished as I told myself I was too focused on my own independently drawn-up call campaigns to focus on Andrew's orders.

Looking back, that is only half the truth. My desk was always a cluttered mess and the notes I took for myself to remind myself of some of Andrew's directions were indecipherable. I could not read my own writing and found myself zoning out even worse than usual as Andrew gave me instructions. Meanwhile, Carlo was perfectly happy with the quality of phone calls I was making, but Andrew on the other hand, was getting fed up with what he perceived as laziness and lack of follow-through.

I could tell by Andrew's voice that he did not feel entirely comfortable in reprimanding me over such things as untimely submission of merchandise orders or lack of perseverance in scheduling appointments with big business advisors. As a coping mechanism, I told myself that I was not threatened by his or anyone else's higher position or status and it was up to me, as it always has been, to distinguish between authority I respected and that which I did not and henceforth would not comply with. Again, this is only half the truth. There were times where I would truly give it my all to fulfill all the merchandise orders and make all the appointments and I still couldn't get my act together. In school, I thought I was too cool; at work, I convinced myself I was too righteous, but in the end, there was still a certain antagonizing perfectionism that I demanded from myself. While I did not believe in what I was doing completely and my psyche was wilting from the perceived meaninglessness of my endeavors, I remained very upset with myself because I did not want to let anyone down, including Andrew. It was time to begin taking Adderall during the day.

I scheduled an appointment with Dr. Van Hove, my childhood psychiatrist, the same doctor who diagnosed me as ADHD at nine years of age. She gladly wrote me a script for 25 mg of Adderall XR (extended release) and another script for 10 mg of instant Adderall for studying in the evening.

* * *

The first week of September represented my first week back on Adderall during the day since junior year of college and it had a noticeable anti-social effect on me. While certainly medication can yield different effects when combined with the unique chemical makeup of one's brain, I found that the medication quashes a certain sociability inherent in my nature. I knew this to be the case, but I rationalized that sacrifice was part of life and part of growing up was giving a little to get a little. Adderall helped my mind to calm down and focus on the same task and did wonders for my merchandise fulfillment success ratio. I told Andrew that I was taking Adderall to assist my efforts in some of the administrative tasks I had proved to be unreliable with in the past. He understood, and admitted that he even took a drug called Straterra to help him with his own mild case of ADD. The more he got to know me, the more he began to recognize my deficits and utilize my strengths. It meant a lot to me as the months went on and he began to tune his voice to sing notes of respect. It made me want to work harder for him, even if it did take me twenty minutes to complete one merchandise order when it took other internals no more than five. The Adderall helped me to endure the extra fifteen minutes necessary to complete the orders.

Unfortunately, it didn't stop with the merchandise. I was bombarded by emails consisting of either directions from Carlo or Andrew, orders or fund inquiries from advisors, marketing procedures and protocol from compliance, and so forth. All of which proved to be more than my scattered mind could handle. I made the decision sometime in mid-September that I would have to earn my CFA Level 1, which normally requires a year's study, in three months to be promoted by early 2007. I needed a secretary to handle my administrative duties so that I could concentrate on the conceptual side of the business. I knew I would thrive in a setting where I could wrestle with concepts and theory all day, and the CFA was my means to get there, and Adderall my ticket.

Chapter 10
Addiction

By late July, following my bump in salary and right to earn commissions since passing the Series 7, I had moved out of my house and into a studio in downtown Manhattan just a few blocks west of Union Square. I chose to live alone despite two offers to room with a couple of my friends. There is something to be said, at least to me, about reigning sovereign over your own territory, and I needed solitude to focus on my studies. By September, I was taking one 25 mg pill of Adderall in the day and a few 25 mg pills at night. It was getting urgent, at least in my own mind, that I pass CFA Level 1 and move up the corporate ladder and find the intellectual stimulation and meaning in my work that I needed. Aside from that, I had rationalized that I needed to be in a position where I could have a secretary to help me with my administrative follies. Looking back, these were some lofty short-term goals. The way I saw it, being a Jew in the shadow of his successful father, if I wasn't chairman of the World Bank by age twenty-seven, or somewhere comparable, then I would be a failure. The fact was, I was not happy, and the Adderall numbed my feelings about the lack of meaning I perceived in finance and allowed me to concentrate on what it would take to advance and mold myself into the ideal of success and wealth.

My life had become fully consumed by my sole purpose to passing the CFA Level 1 in three months. I cut off all social contacts and even my own family, to an extent. The drugs were taking over; I was able to manipulate it so that Dr. Van Hove would write me one prescription for Adderall and my dad would write me another. Before long, my mind was swimming in the artificial pool of insanity that Adderall eventually shaped for me. I would spend the whole night studying some nights and go to work with zero sleep. My coworkers and my boss began to notice the change in me as I became increasingly less participatory in the joking banter I was known to include myself in before I began studying for the CFA. Two things were happening to me: one, I was stressing myself out with the CFA, and two, I was falling deeper into what ultimately turned into a severe problem with Adderall addiction. Luckily, my coworkers and Carlo attributed the perceived change in me only to number one, since the CFA is known to be the most grueling exam in finance with a less than 40 percent pass rate, and this allowed for problem number two to slip under the radar.

Before I go any further I take full responsibility for the Adderall abuse I subjected myself to during those three months of disaster. I was dishonest with both Dr. Van Hove and my father when requesting a new script for the drug, failing to mention to one that I had seen the other and already received a new dose.

On average, I was getting about three hours of sleep a night Sunday through Friday, while crashing for approximately ten hours on Saturday. I began to lose weight, as my appetite had been severely diminished by the Adderall abuse. I was even beginning to lose hair. There were many nights where I didn't bother to have dinner at all, as long as my body received a healthy serving of 30 to 40 mg of instant Adderall on top of the time-released capsule I took in the morning. Food was not a luxury I could afford with the CFA coming up in December; I had precious little time to waste on anything besides studying. It was imperative that I accomplish the impossible, I told myself, and the only way to do this was by living a less-than-healthy existence, if only for the next few months.

My world grew more insane by the day. The skin around my eyes began to develop little red veins and my lower eyelids began to droop. My mind was restless even as my body was sleeping.

Sleep paralysis was not unfamiliar to me, and it came back with a vengeance now. As far back as I can remember, I would occasionally wake to find my body paralyzed as if I was stuck inside a coffin while my mind operated with full awareness. It was one of the few things that could scare me, though I would always inevitably fall back asleep. With the Adderall, I found myself in a dream world of sleep paralysis, never fully knowing whether I was awake or asleep.

I would go to my financial accounting class in mid-October convinced that I was being followed. I would sit in a manic haze as my teacher went over assets, liabilities, and so forth, all the prerequisite knowledge for the CFA exam. I was absorbing nothing and convinced myself that I needed even more Adderall so that I could focus. My instants would run out in a little more than a week's time, since I was taking at least four times the normal dose on a nightly basis. I began to take the time-released Adderall in place of them. The consequences of this decision further contributed to my pre-existing state of delirium, since the time-released Adderall would last anywhere between eight to twelve hours, unlike the instants, which faded after about five hours.

By November I was a malnourished insomniac, yet I still managed to go through the motions of work during the day. I even found an article on real estate investment trusts in *The Economist* that highlighted a couple of our real estate funds. That opportunity ended up turning into a national marketing campaign for Morgan Stanley Investment Management. Looking back, I do not fully understand how I made it through work each day and studied all night for three months straight. My ACT numbers began to drop with each passing month, but I was studying for my CFA, so it was not seen as a big deal at the office.

In late November, I decided that I would meet with a girl my parents had set me up with for brunch in Red Bank, New Jersey. I am normally very hesitant to partake in anything of that nature if my parents have something to do with it, but it was different this time. I remembered this girl from my days at Ranney School. It was Stephanie Jenkins, the girl who used to let me climb into her locker and would subsequently shut the door on me. Mind you, by late November, I was in no shape to charm women after more than two months of heavy amphetamine abuse. We met for breakfast and spoke about various topics of which I cannot recall. I paid for breakfast and we went our separate ways, as I needed to catch a train to New York to get in a full day of studying. Our meeting felt like a dream, my recollection of it foggy and surreal. But my subconscious did pick up on one thing that played back like a video clip: "YOU ARE A VISUAL THINKER."

It was something she said to me casually over breakfast. She was a psychology major and I guess she noticed something. The real question was, why could I not get this point out of my head, especially since I had simply shrugged the idea off as nothing at the time? *Why is this idea about visual thinking such an important revelation?* I thought to myself while sitting back on the train. I did some research and found that visual/spatial thinkers are commonly right-brain-oriented and are often diagnosed with ADHD. I discovered a website by Linda Silverman, PhD, one of the leading pioneers in special education with a focus on the visual thinker. The idea that excited every nerve of my body was the concept of the combination learning disabled and gifted visual thinker, otherwise known as a twice exceptional learner, or as she calls them, "Lost Treasures."

According to Silverman's research, I found that the learning disabled, gifted visual thinkers, the "2e" (twice exceptional) learners, are at high risk in childhood, especially if their learning disability remains undiagnosed. For one, they are able to abstract around their learning disability to the point where the educational system may simply view them as average, or above average at best, in terms of academic performance and intelligence. In other words, their abilities are subdued by their learning disability and their learning disability is never diagnosed due to their counteracting intelligence. The two forces cancel each other out and the school fails to recognize their amazing capabilities. In turn, the student fails to recognize their own capabilities without the positive reinforcement of a system designed for a very different type of thinker and learner.

Silverman discerned that there is a high incidence of auditory processing or auditory inattention problems (something I was diagnosed with) associated with gifted visual thinkers and this is what manifested the idea of this twice exceptional learner in the first place. Often, these children exhibit symptoms of ADD/ADHD due partly to the obvious fact that if a student is not "hearing" what is being said in class, it is logical that they would be more inclined to fidget and day dream while the rest of the class is actually learning.

I distinctly remember the day I was talking to my friend Mike Marulli, who sat next to me at Morgan Stanley, and coincidentally graduated Holmdel High School right before I entered as a freshman, and another friend of mine, Pryah, with whom I also shared a great working relationship. Pryah began asking me questions about the CFA and my mind created some sort of hallucinogenic effect (Adderall-induced, for sure), almost as if to tell me something. Pryah's mouth was moving, but there was a cloud-like visual blocking her mouth and muffling the sound. It looked similar to the censors you might see in front of the mouth of a television character using profanity, but hazier and more surreal. With all the pain and suffering I was putting my brain through at the time, it was evident to me that my subconscious was trying to tell me something. I WAS NOT HEARING A WORD SHE WAS SAYING. It occurred to me later that night, even on the drugs, that perhaps this is something I have always had. As I did more research, I found that auditory processing issues, coupled with thinking in pictures, are also commonly found in autism. I began to wonder if my sense of feeling different and disconnected was attributable to autism. I am not autistic, but I felt connected to this idea because of the common visual mind.

These revelations were not enough to change the course on which I had set myself.

As I fell deeper into addiction, and with the test less than a week away, there were days where my Adderall intake exceeded 100 mg, and one day would speed into the next. I was sacrificing everything for this exam—my friends, my sleep, my sanity. I found myself experiencing emotional highs and lows for seemingly no reason. Luckily, when the situation was at its very worst, I was able to conceal it from the workplace since they had granted me the last week off before the exam to study.

I would lie in my apartment with no sense of time or appetite while my mind hallucinated. I closed my eyes at one point and there was Jesus, illuminated brilliantly with intense coloration and fully multidimensional. As I remember it, he was placing some sort of crown atop his head. It was a true masterpiece as far as psychotic visualizations go. *I'm Jesus!* I felt this rush of euphoria.

I am Jesus! I keep telling myself.

Later that week, I was walking back from Chipotle, one of the few times I had convinced myself that it would be a good idea to nourish myself, when a horizontal beam of yellow light shot into the face of my vision field and literally caused me to lurch back in an attempt to dodge a laser beam of energy. I told myself it had to be the drugs, and chuckled as my heart beat like a drum.

* * *

By the time I arrived at Jacob Javits Center on the west side of Manhattan for the sitting of the CFA Level 1 exam, I was doomed. I hadn't slept in two days and my mind and body were desperately fragile. I lost ten minutes at the beginning after removing the wrong calculator from my backpack. My head was struggling to even read the questions, let alone think and calculate. It was an absolute disaster, though the drugs kept my hope alive through the time-released euphoria that Adderall can be counted upon for.

Following the exam, I found it increasingly harder to get through the day at work. The CFA results were not to be announced for at least a month, and I still had a problem that needed addressing. My parents had finally seen enough change in me that they referred me to a psychiatrist in New York. I went under my own free will as I knew I had a problem that needed to be dealt with.

I admitted to Dr. Jacoby as soon as we sat down together that I had a problem with Adderall. I disclosed to him that there were times where I had consumed over 100 mg on a given day and I hadn't slept like a normal human being since September.

I had even opted not to go out for New Year's Eve, despite numerous invitations to attend various parties.

Dr. Jacoby appreciated my candor and of course recognized immediately that there were some ADHD-like issues that I struggled with, including possible learning disorders which he said he could partially determine from my handwriting on the patient forms. I had never thought of myself as a person with a learning disorder, and I still don't. In fact, I almost resented the term; my sister had been sent to a boarding school for the learning disabled, a term that resonated as nothing more than a home for the children of lazy parents who do not feel like putting forth the effort to raise their own children. I soon learned that being LD is a real phenomenon and can have serious consequences for the children afflicted—and their parents. I later learned that when one sibling faces the challenges that my sister has her entire life, it's natural for parents to shift the burden of success to the other sibling with more ability, or the child most likely to succeed. I see this is a pretty natural response within the family dynamic, and I'm not going to blame my parents for wanting their son to succeed.

Dr. Jacoby decided that despite my problem with Adderall, it was still the best medication for individuals like myself with ADHD and ADHD-like symptoms, so he gave me one more shot at taking the pills responsibly and wrote me a new prescription. I told Dr. Jacoby that the Adderall would no longer be a problem and assured him that my ability to take them under the prescribed dosage, 25 mg a day and 10 mg at night as needed for studying, would not be a question. Interestingly, I had never before struggled with any type of addiction in my life, and maintained that even my experience with Adderall addiction, in my opinion, was not a chemical dependency, but rather a product of the circumstantial context of my life, a context that had not changed even after the CFA exam.

My second episode of Adderall-induced psychosis took place in the third week of January 2007. I could not resist taking two or three instant Adderall instead of one per night. I would come home from work and lay down on the futon in my studio, lonely and discontent with life. I shut friends out and kept myself occupied doing research on a book I had been planning on writing about learning disorders. I felt the that instant Adderall would give me the boost I needed to stay focused on my endeavor, and that quadrupling my prescribed dose would provide me with an even larger boost. I was double-sourcing the Adderall again between two psychiatrists. After months of sleep deprivation on top of everything else I had put my body through in the past months, the situation grew worse. I found myself one night dealing irrationally with the numerical digits of my birth date, and before I knew, it I was reading page 620 (I was born on June 20th) of the Orthodox Jewish Bible, a bizarre choice considering my history. I called my dad, which looking back was probably a subconscious request for help, and told him that I was ready to fulfill my duties as the Messiah, as dictated on page 620 of the Orthodox Jewish Bible. My father cancelled his entire day of seeing patients to drive up with my mother and check on me.

When they arrived, I had already planned my first undertaking as the new Messiah. I proposed to my parents, who sat across the room from me on my kitchen floor, that either George Bush withdraws the troops from Iraq, or he has to watch as a young American dies of hunger in front of his own eyes. There I was, a couple of hours into my hunger strike in defiance of an issue that I was only somewhat ambivalent about. After four hours, my father called the paramedics and even recommended that they bring a few NYPD officers; he knows I can be tough to deal with.

While the whole display was artificially induced by the drugs, and it was true that I did not feel nearly as strongly about the issue of war in Iraq as my declaration would suggest, my father's decision to involve a couple of New York's finest was probably wise. My mother watched over me as I heard the sound of a radio and the hustle of footsteps climbing the stairs like someone had lost track of a herd of buffalo. It took about a fourth of a millisecond just by the sound for me to figure out what was happening. I quickly retreated to my cozy loft overlooking the rest of my studio, the very loft I used to sleep on and wake up in with lumps on my head each morning as a result of the foot and a half of negative space between my nose and the ceiling above. I knew I could buy myself some time up there, since most hefty cops could not be expected to be able to fit up there with me.

I knew from their faces that they were reasonable men and were not looking to incarcerate me, but rather to help me. I told them right away that the last thing I wanted to do was get in a physical showdown with a couple New York City police officers, but that they had no right to barge in and escort me out of the very apartment that I paid for myself. I was not hurting anyone, though as I understand from my studies in political philosophy class, society does have the right to intervene not only when an individual is a threat to others, but also when an individual is a threat to himself. While I did not view it as such at the time, looking back I certainly *was* a threat to myself, and to my parents.

With the assistance of the police and the paramedics, my parents did the right thing. I had the option of cooperating and climbing down from the loft under my own free will or being carried off. While a younger, adolescent me hardly ever backed down from a fight, the last thing I wanted, even in a state of psychosis, was to hit a policeman for obvious reasons, but most importantly because they did not deserve to be hit. My solution was to come down and, as a statement of passive non-compliance, have them cuff me before they walked me out.

My parents were visibly upset by the time I arrived at St. Vincent's emergency room not more than two blocks from my apartment on Twelfth Street and Seventh Avenue. The paramedics and I engaged in friendly conversation on my way over about high school wresting after they noticed the blue Holmdel Wrestling hoodie I had chosen to wear. By the time I climbed out of the ambulance, they had already removed my cuffs, since I was no longer a threat in their eyes. I was pretty cocky about the whole ordeal for a while, until the drugs finally began to wear off. I told the attending psychiatric resident that truly I was not mentally ill and if she would just wait for the drugs to fade, she would be able to see that with her own eyes.

As the hours ticked past, I was beginning to get impatient and even worried that they were going to admit me with some sort of mental disease rather than let me loose. I found out later that one of the diagnoses they were working on before the drug test came back positive was schizophrenia, one disorder I knew for a fact I did not have. The idea was that if I was acting like this without the influence of drugs, then it was more serious. Luckily, I began to come out of it in the nick of time and did not fit the criteria for an overnight stay, though I was given the option to stay. My parents drove me home not long after I was given the okay to leave. The doctor's prognosis was simple: Catch up on my sleep, feed my malnourished body, and never touch Adderall again!

It is not a surprise to me that the country of Canada has already banned Adderall. The drug, while helpful in some respects, is extremely addictive and excessively abused by college students. It has even been known to cause arrhythmia and sudden death. I am lucky to be alive and would encourage the parents of any children on Adderall to monitor them closely should a doctor prescribe it to them to treat the symptoms of ADD/ADHD. My advice is to focus more on what makes these individuals different and unique rather than medicate them to behave like everybody else.

Cases of ADD/ADHD and related disorders have multiplied significantly, even since I was diagnosed around the age of six. Is it fair to call it an epidemic, or can society finally, willingly accept that what we may really be looking at here is an innovative breed of thinking coupled with a certain element of incompatibility with the current system? Many of the ADD/ADHD and LD individuals I have come across exhibit incredible bursts of charisma, creativity, and accomplishment. I, for one, do not wish to suppress any of my own inherent gifts for the sake of an increased ability to focus on things that I frankly do not have any interest in pursuing in the first place. The largest contributor to my problem with Adderall, as I mentioned before, was not chemical by any means. Instead, the abuse spawned from my hard realization that without the artificial impetus that Adderall could provide, I was unable to go through the motions of a life I did not want. That day, while imprisoned for hours inside St. Vincent's, I decided to leave finance and Morgan Stanley.

Chapter 11
Coast to Coast

After much reflection, one thing was all too apparent: I was once again jobless and trapped inside my parents' house. The house itself is beautiful, a monument to my father's hard work and dedication to becoming a successful surgeon. A mother's pride and joy, my father is. He had never been arrested like his son, never struggled academically. Part of me had always wanted to escape the expectations of Jewish young men that my father had thrived under. Another part of me wondered if it was the Jewish element at all that was driving my insane will to succeed. Was it possible that I felt the simple need to please my parents? If I could prove that I was the strong one in the family, my parents could focus more on my sister, who was younger and in need of more attention. I was unsure at the time, of past, present, and future. I had burned through all my options; the harder I had tried to fit the mold, wherever it had come from—a mold I had resisted all of my life—the further I deviated from this ridiculous ideal. And now how was I going to make an upper-six-figure salary sitting at home having resigned from my job at Morgan Stanley, my last shot at the big money? Was this pressure that had built up to a head, all *in* my head?

I had always been rebellious, so why was this bothering me so much? If I *wanted* to be this cookie-cutter, well-behaved robot, I suppose I could have made that choice. To be honest, the only way to battle nature, as man has figured out, is through technology. Adderall was technology for my brain. But experience has taught us, again, that man can only hope to contain nature—not conquer it. I certainly didn't feel experienced. Since moving back to my childhood home from New York City, I felt like a child, not fully registering what I had been through.

I impulsively chose to give the doctor gig one last try, being that I only had two classes left to qualify for med school. I rationalized that of the three options every good Jewish boy may choose from to make it big, being a doctor represented the most altruistic. It would not be hard to derive meaning from such work, and it would provide me with the opportunity to make a good living.

I saw Dr. Jacoby again in New York, and to my amazement, he offered me another stimulant: Ritalin, which is used to treat ADHD-type symptoms. It helped. After a couple weeks of Chemistry II at the local community college, I was at least passing, but it did not take long for me to begin abusing Ritalin. I would lock myself in my room and stare blankly at the chemistry textbook and convince myself to increase my dosage. I had taken organic chemistry already, but had failed Chemistry II at Tulane, the supposed prerequisite to organic. Oh well. In any case, my mind was speeding, and the only truly interesting concept I took to heart was that of entropy, which in my mind equaled out to this idea of increasing universal chaos, to which my wandering soul could relate. Chaos, interconnected universal forces, maybe God—call it what you will.

I was so high on Ritalin as I drove home from my summer class one day that I found myself wondering if my mind was still in my brain or if it was out in the sky rendering reality just a brief second before I would travel through it. I perceived that the way things were going, my escapism was at a pinnacle moment. I was never going to be a doctor. I wondered if Jesus really *had* visited me that day in my Manhattan apartment just before going to the hospital.

I arrived home and saw my mom standing by the front door. She said Harold Sylvester had left a message and wanted to speak to me about a show he wanted to produce based upon a portion of a book I had written (an early edition of the book

you are reading now). Harold is a Tulane alumnus and Emmy
Award-winning actor and writer, but I knew him as Griff from
Married With Children. I had figured it would be a long shot,
but that he would possibly take a look at an unfinished version of
my manuscript, so I sent it. He was gracious and agreed to read
what I had written. A month went by and I had forgotten that
he had a copy until my mother explained to me with enthusiasm
and pride that he had just flown back from Europe and wanted
to speak to me that night.

I called him at eight and the first words out of his mouth,
having just read through my writing in raw form, were, "Brian.
Hey man, let me tell you . . ." I waited with eager anticipation.
"You are one piece of work."

I just started cracking up. It was a laugh I really needed at
the time. We talked from there about creating characters for a
show based upon my view of the world and specifically my two
Tulane chapters. He had grown up in the projects and was the
country's first African American scholarship recruit, and though
our experiences at Tulane were very different, our perspectives
were surprisingly similar. He went on to explain that he, too,
was one of those creative right-brained visual thinkers and that
I ought to move to LA and work on this project with him.

He stated boldly, "Brian, I don't really think you want to be
a doctor."

To which I responded, and keep in mind I was still high on
Ritalin at the time, "Well maybe, but I feel like I might be able to
invent something one day, or elaborate on string theory, maybe
develop the physical theory of everything."

He was quiet after that response, not knowing fully whether
I was serious or not. I internalized my own laughter and
wondered the same thing. Then I told him I needed to think
about his offer.

I called my high school buddy Rob Pepitone the next day
and told him I was moving to LA in a week and offered him a
chance to come along. Rob had spent the last couple of months
meditating and growing a garden in his parents' backyard, and I
knew the kid needed a change. I figured California was more his
vibe and he agreed it was time to get out of Holmdel.

My silver four-door was so completely stuffed with both

of our belongings that we literally had no view out the rear windshield. The car felt heavy as I backed out a couple feet, only to smash into some sort of immovable object—Rob's brother's girlfriend's car. I assured Chris' girlfriend that I'd pay for the damages and we were on our way. Goodbye New Jersey, goodbye pre-med, goodbye psychiatrists, goodbye convention. It was time to step into a different realm.

* * *

I had printed out a MapQuest just before grabbing Rob. We tore through northwestern New Jersey crossing the Delaware Water Gap into Pennsylvania doing one hundred miles per hour heading west on Interstate 80. Rob was a bit anxious at first and nibbled on his jar of figs, but the tension soon eased. We made our first stop somewhere west of Cleveland at a Motel 8. Ohio, to me, still felt too close—mentally, at least—in terms of pushing into my future. Ohio reminded me of Molly and her childhood home outside Cleveland that I had visited a few times, and Molly was still a touchy subject.

We awoke early the next morning and skipped breakfast, determined to hit the road hard. The yellow of Ohio transitioned into the light green of Indiana by the afternoon. Before we knew it, Gary was in our rearview mirror as we crossed into Illinois. I gave Molly a call letting her know we were not far outside of Chicago, her current city of residence, and she eagerly invited us to stop in and say hello.

From farmland to urban metropolis, Chicago manifested itself within our consciousness from a distance, a faded image of buildings tall and packed amongst each other like some sort of exclusive high school clique. As we came closer, the city felt as if it was above us, rather than in front of us. If I hadn't known New York as well as I did, I might have been more impressed by its magnitude, but it was still the largest city we were going to pass through until LA. We picked a random street heading in the direction of the heart of the city and parked. We ended up paying ten dollars to keep our car in a lot downtown. In New York, it would have been triple that.

Molly ended up bailing in accordance with her boyfriend's wishes, but her friend Debbie met with Rob and me, and we taxied it over to the artsy district where she was more than hospitable, offering us a place to stay for the night and grabbing dinner with us followed by a rendezvous at one of her neighborhood bars. I wasn't completely upset at Molly, but I was a bit hurt that she had invited us, only to flake out at the last second. She is ADHD like I am, and I understand that we sometimes act impulsively. She told me later that she knew I would have started up with her boyfriend. She may have had a point. In any case, Debbie and I got drunk together into the early morning.

I woke up the next morning to hear Rob and Debbie babbling about something in a far-off room, and I gathered up our things. We hit the road heading west, brushing briefly over the border of Wisconsin before heading into Iowa, the real garden state. Iowa, to me, was one of the grandest stretches of road and landscape I have ever seen, a plush saturated green that was nearly hypnotizing at the peak of late-summer sunlight. I felt as if time was nonexistent and only temperature and light governed the existence of the rolling farmland that seemed to extend out into infinity. We stopped at a gas station to fill up and grab some spicy beef jerky. I gave the land around me an intensely focused look through my mind's eye. I felt like I was literally in a geographic vacuum, as if the space-time continuum had not fully resolved itself, and yet here I was leaning against my car in Iowa. Or maybe it was me who had not resolved myself, and the vacuum was of the mind—a place of no time, and no space, but only consciousness. For a moment, there was no past and no future, only the stillness of a psyche that was free to wander.

We loaded back in the car and by evening we had crossed over the Nebraskan border. "Welcome to the Good Life," the sign read. I guess if the good life is in Nebraska, then we really had no reason to drive all the way to LA, but something told me to push on. When we displaced ourselves from the lush green of Iowa and returned to the universe's regularly scheduled space-time experience, Rob and I were both a bit disappointed at the landscape's return to yellowish brown, as if we were back in Ohio. Fortunately, our perception changed as the sun began to dip and we were treated to the most divine sunset; there were colors you could only dream of. The Nebraska sky literally made us feel like we were stoned out of our minds, the only difference being that I was driving just fine. It began to rain just as the sun fully disappeared and the aromas of the farmland revealed themselves in true olfactory bliss. Then we looked up at the clearest sky I will ever see. Nebraska *was* the good life, I thought as I began to see signs for Denver popping up, but I knew it was never going to be my life, as good is a relative term, and what's good is not always what's right. To me Nebraska was good, but certainly not right for me.

Rob began to doze off as we crossed into Colorado. We swiped through the city of Denver as I began to wonder where in the hell were the legendary Rocky Mountains. The defining and monumental moment of truly reaching the "West" began in my mind at the beginning of our ascent into the Rockies, and before I had time to obsess over the notion, my car was suddenly pointed about 45 degrees closer to the sky, and I could feel the magnitude of the enormous bulge beneath my tires.

Neuro-stimulated liberation rushed through my veins and into my head as I knocked the manual transmission back a gear to handle the incline. I felt like I had reached the next frontier of my life, from an old boy to a young man. I drove with the sense that I was now in control of my life, leaving New Jersey and its expectations behind. The West represented freedom to me, and I wasn't even thinking about Los Angeles, as we still had a lot of road ahead, but I felt as if I could finally look ahead through my own two eyes, without a community of approving or even disapproving eyes looking back at me. I was in control, and life expands with courage to take control, a lesson only learnable through experience.

It was around one in the morning when we stopped at some random exit to stock up on energy drinks and snacks and get some much-needed shuteye. Rob and I both reclined our seats as much as possible, which was only about a half an inch, considering the cargo load behind us. Rob fell asleep instantly as I struggled to even close my eyes. I felt an impulsive inspiration to reach Utah by sunrise. I spent the next five or so hours tearing through the Rockies. The feeling was a cross between

Disney World's Space Mountain and Germany's Autobahn. I was weaving speedily through the dark, dipping and rising, as the Rocky Mountains became my conquerable entity. As the landscape began to flatten out for a bit, I saw signs indicating that I was closing in on the next set of mountains terrain, and the beginning of Utah.

Rob awoke just as we crossed over the border, literally shocked. Picture traveling through Nebraska, the last bit of light we had known at the time, falling asleep, not very far into a pitch-black Colorado, only to awaken in Utah surrounded by the dark red mountainous plateaus representing the next variant of the Rockies. We passed an exit shortly after the border labeled the Trail Through Time, and I almost stopped to check it out until I reminded myself that my journey thus far, and that which remained ahead, was my own trail through time. About ten minutes later, I pulled to the side of the road, snapped a photo of the sun rising behind us, and switched to the passenger side for some much-needed rest. Rob took the wheel and we decided to detour off the linear path we had mapped to check out Arches National Park. We were once again weaving our way through the mountains.

We were about twenty minutes into our tangential adventure when I asked Rob to stop the car. We were on a bridge with what I believed to be the Colorado River below us, and I was almost paralyzed by the natural beauty around me. Looking through my panoramic scope, I saw a bridge not too far off in the distance paralleling the one we were standing on. Beyond that and simultaneously behind me, and really all around me, were the magnificent red iron oxide cliffs. It was unreal. As my head gyroscoped around once more, I caught a glimpse of a pair of docked canoes near a group camping on the small portion of beach-like terrain tracing part of the river.

The park turned out to be gigantic, spanning 119 square miles. We drove around from arch to arch, stopping in various spots to go hiking. Rob was prepared to scale some tough angles with his sneakers. I ended up tossing my sandals to the side to climb barefoot, thereby eliminating slippage. My feet gained traction nicely against the dry and somewhat sandy rock as I met Rob atop a solid forty-foot mound. We then moved to the edge of a cliff looking out over what must have been a thousand-foot drop. Numerous stacks of rock, each with about four or five in number, were placed on top of each other in ascending order by size as the formations rose vertically. I supposed these piles of rock symbolized some sort of territorial mark of trespass for those who had made it to that point prior to our arrival. Alternatively, it could have been some sort of ancient Native American tribute to the gods. To me, they symbolized bravery, and I scanned the ground for quite a while looking for the piece that would serve as the foundation to my own pile of rocks. I found a few other pieces rather quickly after that, and capped my project off with a pyramidal top piece, and walked away. I subsequently sat down, dangling my legs over the cliff as I took in the endless view of valleys and mountains.

When we left Utah, Rob was adamant about the "energy" of the mountains. I agreed with him, as the magnitude of their presence was irresistibly emotive. But something about the obviousness of the statement made me laugh at him. I instantly felt a pain in my heart as I knew I hurt his feelings. I knew Rob was brilliant, but decades away from being the Buddhist master he thought himself to be. (He would definitely get there, though.) As we carried on through the desert we tore through a piece of Arizona just before hitting Nevada. The landscape really didn't change much from there on, with the Rockies to our right rolling past just as fast I was driving, albeit in the opposite direction. It was summer in the hottest geographical section of the US; the air was thirsty and the desert consumed our imaginations. We had been almost two thousand miles in two and a half days and my car deserved a rest, as even camels need water from time to time.

At the edge of my perception and the foggy haze of the scalding heat, there was an oasis—a mirage, perhaps, derived from my wild imagination, though I wasn't on drugs at the time. No, it was for real. Las Vegas materialized like an industrial bubble atop an infinite plane of steam and light. We headed straight for it and Rob and I split a sixty-dollar room about a mile off the main strip. We walked toward the casinos, conversing with a homeless man for a good portion of our walk. The entire time he was trying to sell us a rose for our girlfriends, only the rose was missing a petal or two, much like the man himself. We hit the Hard Rock Hotel after a brief taxi ride, where Rob and I decided to try our luck with the casinos. I lost twenty dollars almost instantaneously on the slots and made eighty back in a couple rounds of blackjack. I could tell Rob thought gambling was a sin of some sort, according to his ever-changing moral philosophy, and was rooting against me secretly so that I'd learn my lesson. I'd say I've learned enough lessons in my day, and that some things were just never going to change; for instance, my intrigue with anything involving risk and the supposed unconquerable. Not to say that blackjack qualifies as unconquerable, but the speed at which we reached Vegas leaving from Jersey not so many afternoons ago I'd reckon would be tough for anyone to beat.

* * *

With the flashing lights and the constant temptations, I felt the impulsive ADHD chaos streaming through my veins once again, perhaps overstimulated, and that was before I began drinking at the Steele Pulse concert outside by the pool. I remember downing a few Vodka Red Bulls to try and keep pace, having driven all night through Colorado only to spend the day hiking in Utah. The *who* and the *where* of what I am were streaming back and forth in an almost circular pattern.

We ended up crashing until about eleven the next morning, prepared mentally for the last leg of our trip across the country. LA was theoretically about five hours away. The landscape was much the way it had been since Arizona, and I could feel we were getting close. When we hit the California inspection at the border, I felt a surge of excitement and euphoria. The female officer asked us quickly if we were harboring any illegal produce, which looking back was a pretty hilarious question. No, we were not harboring any illegal "produce," or even weapons of mass destruction, just a little bit of LSD. We carried on and intentionally passed the exit for Hollywood so that I-10 would dwindle down past exit one and we would have no choice but to introduce our presence to the Pacific, the monument of the end our trip. Dark blue and marvelous, gleaming in the sunlight, I snapped a photograph. We had arrived.

Chapter 12
Hollywood

Rob and I had just torn through the country with a feel for the landscape that one can only obtain by driving state by state and mental state by mental state. We were exhausted as we found the studio apartment I had impulsively chosen without regard to its exact geographical whereabouts. It was in Hollywood, that was really all that mattered, and my mind felt like it had just gone through some sort of time warp to get there. Not far north of us were the hiking trails of Runyon Canyon. My perception of self at that point was in flux, having traveled so far to reach a destination I knew nothing about. I had resolved myself, however, to get a good feel for the city, and even if I were to move out of Hollywood, to stay in California—most likely closer to the beach in Santa Monica, now that I think about it.

In Hollywood, the phonies were numerous and easily identifiable, but there really was something to the genuine characters found in the area. Of all the stereotypes surrounding Hollywood—for instance, "everything is phony," "nothing is real," or my favorite, "the land of the crazy people"—were simultaneously true and, ultimately, false. If the world is just an image within my mind, as it has been scientifically proven that there is no absolute proof of a world outside of your own head, then what is reality to begin with? If that is such a crazy notion, then perhaps I am a little crazy. Out here in Hollywood, the "crazy" people, for those who really understand the situation, are considered artists, writers, actors, and so forth. They are human, many of them just trying to get by on their talent within one of the most competitive industries in the world—the entertainment business.

I, for one, was not caught up in the potential success of this new project of mine, as I was still unsure whether I cared about success as society would view it, and was pretty much convinced at the time that, at 2,700 miles away from home, the last thing I was going to do was let this idea of accumulating wealth and the mentality that goes with it follow me after working so hard and fast to get the hell out of the Northeast. Really, it was a nice situation for all of us. My parents took comfort in the fact that their son was out in LA working with Mr. Harold Sylvester, Emmy Award-winner, and I was just happy to once again discover and wander through new realms. And, of course, I was aware that there was business to take care of.

I called Harold up a few days after I arrived and we made plans for me to travel up to North Hollywood, which is in the valley, not too far from where I was living. I was excited to meet Harold, but not the least bit intimidated. I was just thrilled that someone of such talent had recognized my abilities, and furthermore, from our conversation a couple weeks prior, I knew we were like-minded. I remember I had made it to his house in plenty of time, taking into consideration that I had no idea where I was without the directions I had copied from MapQuest. The traffic in LA was as reflectively insane and chaotic as the people inhabiting the city.

When I pulled into Harold's neighborhood, it felt blandly suburban, with modest houses, all of them rather similar, efficiently spaced out along the sidewalk—except for one, which I knew without looking was Harold's house. It was partially fortified behind two beautiful fences lined with green shrubbery. There was no gate, per se, as the driveway was U-shaped, allowing people and automobiles to enter and exit freely. But the fence stood for prominence, as if to say, there better be a good reason for you to pass through. Luckily, I had my ticket.

I parked on the curb out of respect as I normally do when I visit anyone and walked over the grass, passing through the looped driveway rather than around it. I was a bit lost at first; I wasn't sure if I was to enter through the front door of his house. I gave him a call to let him know I had arrived, and he told me to come to his office, which stood adjacent to the house, looking like a smaller version of the house itself. This was the American Dream. He had a nicely sized piece of land (not cheap in Southern California) with a rather large white wooden-paneled house with green shutters.

I was about thirty feet from his office when he came out to greet me. Neither of us said a word to each other in the midst of the drama of my approach. I recall seeing him evaluate me in a hard glance. All the while, I was wondering if he thought me to be a Nazi, with my newly shaved head and sideburns. I had been shaving my head on and off since eighth grade.

I extended my hand out to greet him and asked him in a cool manner, "Hey man, how ya doing?"

He responded in an even cooler manner, "Hey Brian, getting old."

We subsequently went inside and sat down on the couch, where I noticed a silver plate with a partially smoked cigar laying on top as if to radiate success. We sat on the couch and instantaneously began to talk about how both of us had struggled with society's conception of our own identities. I went on to explain how I had literally beat the shit out of individuals on occasion who ever dared call myself or any of my friends a kyke. My friend Blake could certainly attest to that, as I think back to a specific altercation in a pizza joint in New York's West Village.

It was clear to me that we both cared deeply for the people we supposedly belonged to, though at his point in life he was probably more comfortable with his own feelings on the subject than me. Harold struck me as a proud man and a free man with many achievements to back it up, including being the first black NCAA Division I scholarship athlete for basketball, on top of his success as an actor in the cutthroat entertainment industry. He had a role in *An Officer and a Gentleman* and played Griff on *Married With Children*. As a writer, he had been given high praise for the made-for-TV movie *Passing Glory*. He wrote a few episodes for *NYPD Blue* and had even won an Emmy for his role as producer of the documentary *On Hallowed Ground*.

When we sat down at his desk, his son Harold joined us as we began to look at the characters I had drawn up for the pilot we were about to begin working on. In between work, Harold Sr. told me about his younger days, when he used to attend Black Panther rallies and get tear-gassed from time to time.

He told me simply, "I was a radical, just like you."

He fought for civil rights the way I would have fought in his position, not with peaceful integration into a system that was clearly oppressive and lacked true acknowledgement of the needs of black people in those days, but under the threat of radical change by any means necessary. I don't know the exact details of what went down in those days, though I doubt he ever laid a hand on anybody, unless somebody came at him the wrong way. I see the public school system in the same manner. Just because most kids in school fit a certain mold does not mean that they have the right to deny the many gifted kids falling through the cracks. This very idea equates to the denial of opportunity. From a black man's perspective, I would have fought with passion during the civil rights movement because where there is oppression, there is tyranny, and submissive obedience will never get the job done in such a situation. Not in society, and not in the classroom.

Harold, in his late fifties, the man sitting in front of me, was a true hero in my eyes, and I was honored to be in his presence. Despite all the passion I know he possesses, he is one of the coolest and laid-back individuals I have ever met. No Hollywood attitude or sense of entitlement, just mutual respect. I left that day feeling my whole world had shifted gears. Harold Sylvester, no matter when or if our project comes to fruition, did me a great favor. If not for him, I would have still been abusing nasty ADHD drugs in a frustrating attempt to live up to the standards of being a nice Jewish boy—even if those efforts were drug-fueled. Harold showed me that personal freedom is possible, and to him I am very grateful, though I am still on my own quest to find within me what he eventually found within himself.

* * *

I came to learn that the entertainment business really is nothing like any other business, especially Wall Street, where everything happens with intense speed and direct, linear responses. Hollywood, I soon realized, is not the type of business one should ever attach expectations to in terms of a timetable. Just as my intuitive sense is that time is a man-made invention ordered for the sake of scheduling ourselves, I think Hollywood, or LA for that matter, may be the only place on earth that actually abides by the notion of timelessness. The sun will shine without any real sense of seasons, and meanwhile, everyone is just trying to get their project noticed. Even Harold, an established artist with success and a little bit of fame, could not simply push a button to get a show on TV.

I had just moved to Hollywood when a writers' strike came to fruition, which proved to be an extremely frustrating time for me. Harold and I couldn't make progress with our project, let alone present it. I took to smoking a lot of wonderfully potent pot and drinking as I've always done. The pot in LA was incredible, and much of it was straight out of Uncle Sam's laboratory—medicinal marijuana, the legal type found only in California. I had liquidated my 401(k), which was pretty stacked after a year at Morgan Stanley. All my money was in emerging markets, and ended up providing me with about six months of rent without having to get a job. Looking back, it was the wrong way to go about things, because I have been known to be quite self-destructive when my day—as it did every day—revolved around Hindu Kush (weed) and beer of all varieties. Socially I was my usual self, scattered among various groups, including the potheads living above me, a pretty girl named Megan down the hall, and a few on-and-off girlfriends. I was basically procrastinating until I needed to get a job, typical of someone with ADHD, but considering the amount of money I was spending on alcohol, there was clearly more going on.

I was considerably depressed, having moved out to the opposite coast where I knew nobody. The furniture in my studio consisted of a futon mattress and the bongo left behind by Rob when he flew back to Jersey. I was considerably alone, feeling much like I did during my days in New York, where I was wrapped in depression and isolated. I would take a lot of walks and work on the project here and there, but everything was moving so slowly and I felt empty living and spaced out under the eternal sunshine of Los Angeles. I began to hike Runyon Canyon between, occasionally socializing with people I knew I could never really let in as friends, and drinking myself silly. Hiking was probably the one healthy endeavor I had insisted upon. I would hike up what is probably about a good mile and a half in altitude over terrain tiered similarly to the Great Wall of China, though of course lacking the brick composition. I lost a lot of weight after committing myself to hiking up and then trekking down the canyon three times a week. It was beautiful at the top on a clear day. Looking west, you can see the Santa Monica Mountains stretching out into the Pacific Ocean; straight ahead is Hollywood, and looking east you can see Downtown LA. At the very top point of the mountain, you are literally above it all, as if LA is some sort of foreign object down below.

As I looked down, my depression grew deeper. I was still fairly new in the city, and the project was stalled indefinitely due to the writers' strike. It wasn't the worst situation, so I was wondering why I still wasn't happy. Perhaps it was because even with all the distance I put between myself and the money-chasing mentality I thought I had to embrace to make the family proud, I was still logically in the same situation. I was fully expected to make it huge in Hollywood, an industry worth billions. I had a phone call with my dad a few days before where he told me I'd be the next Larry David, easily worth a couple hundred million in a few years. I appreciated his confidence in me, but was it misplaced? I resolved that I would not return to the Northeast, not even for a visit, before I made it big. At least that was one side of my story in California.

I began to see LA as a place for drifters, and I felt like a drifter myself. I loved just chilling out on a park bench at the top of Runyon Canyon, or near the sand in Venice Beach. My friend Ashley told me about a band of counter-culture rebel rich kids in Venice; born into wealthy families; they had chosen to disown all the privilege and expectations of the scripted life. They literally chose to be homeless on the street under the warmth of the Venice sun.

I already knew what it was like to be homeless, at least for a while, in China, in frigid weather, and I found it to be one of my most awakening and life-affirming days. *Maybe I should be homeless for a while with the hippies at Venice beach,* I mused. Obviously, homelessness is not all that it's cracked up to be, but I figured maybe I wanted to really suffer and see what it was like to sink to the bottom. This was right around the time my friend Justin Schanzer flew in to visit. I picked him up at the airport and put the homeless idea on hold for a bit as I showed him the various sights of Hollywood and the surrounding LA area. I even agreed to meet some of his friends for Shabbat dinner, just to see how I would react after all these years. We ended up meeting a few of his buddies at some sort of Hebrew school where all these Orthodox Jews were chanting one of my least favorite languages. I met the rabbi in charge of rounding up the young LA Jews in the community and he immediately attempted to hand me a yamaka, which I declined. The others kind of gave me a look, but Justin knew what to expect. I told the rabbi, "I do not want to disrespect you, and if that is the case then I will leave." He gave me an evaluating glance and told me no, I would not be disrespecting him.

We sat for about twenty minutes as they recited prayers out of the Torah as I silently scanned the room, half daydreaming, half aware of the five rabbis who approached the table in consecutive order in two-minute increments, placing yamaka after yamaka on my table. With each yamaka, the rabbi I was with took them and placed them under his prayer book. After the prayer session, we went back to his house, where his wife had cooked up a true feast at the dinner table. In between bites, I remained silent as the rest of the table recited prayers, though there was one thing different about this Shabbat dinner from the last Shabbat dinner I had attended ten years ago—we all took shots of Jack Daniels in between prayers, which certainly helped to ease my anxiety, considering the context of my whereabouts and with the weight of my principles. As the night went on, I watched as the others continued to recite prayers here and there as we all moved on to single-malt Scotch.

Perhaps a little Jack was exactly what I needed to withstand Hebrew school back in the day, which is what I pronounced to the rabbi as the dinner carried on. I began to debate with him about how people were killing each other over religion, and if we could all only abide by a code of ethics *un*attached to some sort of supernatural deity, we would no longer feel the need to kill in the name of this or that "God." Jesus, for instance, preached peace and honor; meanwhile, how many millions of people have been murdered in his name, all the while representing the polar opposite of everything Jesus stood for? Religion, as I saw it, was truly the anti-Christ, the root of all evil alongside greed, and the differences between the two are difficult to distinguish. We went back and forth for a while, all the while taking shots of whiskey, to end the night. I left very grateful for what turned out to be an interesting and most delicious evening. I had nothing but respect for the rabbi as he tried to invite me back for next Shabbat dinner. I told him he can count on me in another ten years from that very date. We compromised on five.

Later that week, my new friend Dave introduced me to a girl running trips to Israel. Basically, every Jewish young adult under the age of twenty-six can sign up for a free ride under a program called Birthright Israel. I told her I was the kid who always got suspended in Hebrew school for lashing out and that I certainly doubted I would enjoy myself on some sort of religious tour through the "homeland."

She smiled and told me, "Yeah, I remember the kids like you. They were always the most sensitive ones."

I suppose she was right. Despite the tough-guy attitude and the conviction that nothing affects me and everyone is stupid, I suppose I was a little bit sensitive. I had learned to block out my emotions, and in doing that, my sensitivity toward the world has often translated into thunderous outbursts of discontent and anger. She was right, but I still wasn't signing up.

Chapter 13
Rehab

The drinking worsened with time to the point where my studio apartment gleamed with sunshine refracting through mounds of empty bottles piled in the kitchen and hallway. A young man whose life revolves around bottles of Trappist monk–brewed Chimay and benzodiazepines to keep him down was probably going to bottom out sometime soon, especially with the assistance of the cocaine given to him by a wacko psychiatrist in his Hollywood apartment overlooking Santa Monica Boulevard. Among the white blaze of cocaine looping through his synapses, there was a shining moment of clarity.

"Dad, I'm all coked up, and constantly wasted, and have been for the last nine months or so. I should probably go to rehab."

"Okay, Bri, your plane leaves tomorrow. We love you."

The psychiatrist had warned me that coke is addictive as if he wrote me a script for a take-home regimen and added that I needed to comply with the proper medicinal guidelines associated with the distribution of a controlled substance. I smiled as I bumped another line.

"See ya, Doc," I answered in a hyped-up trance.

"Sure," he replied, "I'll see you around, I'm sure."

"Nope, you won't. I'm heading to rehab."

Goodbye Hollywood!

* * *

I was in the mountainous terrain of outer Tucson. Coyotes howled in the background, the new backdrop to the latest update of my reality. The sound, far from my four walls, added to the feeling that here, I was safe from myself. They drug-tested me, even though I had already disclosed to them every drug I had taken in the past few months, consisting of medicinal marijuana and cocaine, but never heroin, as much as I would have liked to have tried it once. Rehab would have to be a one-time thing, and I would therefore never have the opportunity to do heroin.

I walked around during my first day with needles lodged in my socks pricking the skin on my ankles and shins as a result of walking into a few cactus plants during my preliminary exploration of my new home. There was a green band around my wrist indicating that I was a voluntary patient in a drug and alcohol rehabilitation facility. I looked around at the people who were ostensibly in the same position as me, and I couldn't relate to them. These people had problems. I was just passing time. Living like I was living was a choice; I didn't need to drink, and didn't even crave it when I wasn't. I wasn't weak like these people, and these people would never be my friends. We were nothing alike.

I showed up to my fist counseling session thinking that it was a classroom of sorts. Lizzy the social worker, assigned to me and a few others, was a sweet old British lady to whom I took an instant liking. She had me introduce myself to the group, which consisted of two girls from Houston. One of them was Mary, a pretty blond suck-up, investment banking type who had just finished up work on her MBA and was on extended leave from Merrill Lynch. She had her redeeming qualities, but her clear lack of core self-identity left her with a personality she'd let you peel off willingly, as with an onion, where the layers disintegrate with a simple cut and you are left with a foul stench and stinging eyes. The other girl from Houston was more interesting. Lauren was overweight and unattractive, with an eating disorder and an alcohol problem. She was later determined to suffer from anti-social personality disorder, which is the latest euphemism for sociopath, I think. I'd say her clear disregard for the feelings of others came off as much more genuine than the overdone, superficial attempts that Mary would put forth, like a Girl Scout who traded in her merit badges for a six-figure income, a wardrobe exclusively designed by J.Crew and Polo, and a two-bedroom condo away from the "dredges of society" as she put it.

Still, I despised almost everything about Lauren, and I struggled with great difficulty not to lose my composure when I found out eight months later that she broke her neck and died after falling down her stairs in her condo wasted on wine and half a bottle of Ambien. Apparently, she had hated herself beyond anyone else's worst opinion of her. This was a sad girl, and I should have been nicer to her.

My initial days at Sierra Tucson were difficult for me, as I was having a tough time complying with all the rules. I was uncooperative during the large meetings where everyone would listen to the various updates and newsworthy events prefacing the upcoming week of activities and therapy sessions. These were the same meetings where we would end in a gigantic circle and beg God to "help us to accept the things we cannot change." I would not step in the circle, and I was certainly not going to partake in a mass chant like a member of a cult.

I told my Jewish friend Sam about my hesitation to join the circle, since I wasn't sure about God to begin with. He slapped me forcibly over the head an open palm as if to suggest that there is something higher than my own existence. I guess I always supposed there might be, but it never actually hit me like that. Still, I refused. I was lost in a maze of my own design. While I wasn't attending the AA meetings, since they were too religious, I *was* attending the group counseling sessions with the social worker. It was all helpful, to an extent. I still felt trapped and I was sorry I made the call about rehab to my father while under the influence. Deep down I knew I could control myself. I had put myself here voluntarily, perhaps to delay growing up, because I didn't like people who were "grown up." I didn't want to be that person.

As if via parachute, I began to descend into the idea that maybe this place could be of some use. I was there, and insurance was paying for it, so I might as well "find myself" or something.

I began to introspect at the social work group meetings. We discussed triggers, meaning what situations or scenarios would typically lead us to abuse alcohol. I mentioned that I had been livid over the writers' strike in Hollywood starting before I even had a chance to work on my project. I spoke about the pressures of growing up with high expectations and how I honestly felt like I could meet them in some way, but I haven't succeeded yet. I was drinking like never before due to my perceived failure in LA.

I took up smoking for the six weeks I was there, and we'd all sit in the smoking hut during down-time and discuss whatever came to mind. I would listen to some of the heroin addicts discuss the way their veins would throb sometimes when they just spoke about getting high. Another guy said he would dress in formal attire before he would pop Ambien by the handful. He wanted to look his best for the drug. I really appreciated the candor of the people around me, which allowed me to open up a little myself. I began to admit I had an anger problem rather than an alcohol problem, and that living felt like war to me since about nineteen years old. I admitted that I could be recklessly impulsive at times, and that it had cost me on occasion. I felt lost, I confessed, like I was floating in an ocean with only a semblance of direction, even if it was me who chose to willingly depart from shore.

A couple weeks in, I had an appointment with a holistic psychologist. That's the best way I can describe this woman, as her actual title escapes me. She asked what makes me anxious and why I needed to cover it with alcohol. I told her, to be honest, it was scenarios like this, where someone looks at me face-to-face and our eyes meet through conversation. If I'm still and sitting directly across from you, I know there is only a minute chance that I'm not going to space out on you, and your words will evaporate.

She stared at me and asked, "What is the true rhythm of the earth?" I looked at her, perplexed. She asked me again, "What is the speed, what is the nature of the sound?"

I took a guess. "Slow and deep?"

"Exactly. Slow and deep. So, when you are anxious because you think you are going to lose focus, I want you to listen to the rhythm of the earth, and center yourself. Now, I want you to picture yourself under a waterfall. The waterfall is showering you with yellow energy. Now breathe in." I breathed in. "When you breathe in I want you to breath in the yellow light, the positive energy, and when you breathe out, I want you to picture yourself breathing out the darkness, the negativity. Breathe the yellow light in, and breathe the darkness out. Your mind is on overdrive. You need to slow it down."

I try to do this exercise every time I need to focus and cannot seem to. It has been helpful, and it's something I never would have considered had I not met this unique psychologist with mermaid-red hair and an unbreakably intense demeanor.

The day after that meeting, we were taken to interact with horses on a ranch on the outer grounds of the facility. It was the first time I had ever encountered these majestic creatures, and they taught me a lot in a short amount of time. We were not riding them, but simply standing with them and guiding them with ropes. I learned that you cannot pull a horse in any desired direction, especially with impatience. You must first let the horse approach you, let it sniff you out, and then you can suggest a change in direction once the trust has been established. It will not go somewhere merely because you want it to, but rather, it senses when you are offering it a choice, and then it will follow. It's a great lesson about how to approach the things you want in life. Sometimes the less you desire, and the more freedom you give to something or someone to respond, the higher the likelihood that you will achieve what you are seeking.

For so long I was putting forth an unrefined aggression instead of plotting over time. Raw ADHD energy has to be harnessed and channeled the right way, something I was not doing well. I decided to apply this not only to the things I want to achieve, but to people in general. I needed to give people the benefit of the doubt more often, and not just pull them into my own prefabricated assumption about them, where my expectation of them to disappoint becomes a self-fulfilling prophecy. Expectations are powerful.

The more I got to know the people around me, the more I began to accept my situation. Most of the people around me had either ADHD, OCD, bipolar disorder, or any combination of these. Interestingly, they were also some of the most successful and creative people I've ever met. There were CEOs, Navy SEALs, entrepreneurs, lawyers, doctors, and of course, people in the entertainment business. This is not what comes to mind when you think "rehab," but here we were, all together at last. These were people with immense talent, and real problems. One of my friends was a physics major in college who started a multi-million-dollar media company. He'd take breaks from his success to smoke crack. Another was the son of a major producer in Hollywood with his own film aspirations who lost his sense of reality after dropping acid one too many times.

It was eye-opening to be around people like this—people who had achieved success unconventionally. Many of them were not straight-A students—some even struggled with school—but they were enormously accomplished. The greatest part of rehab, besides just giving my mind and body a break from ill-conceived substances, were the spiritual revelations inherent in living in a desert for six weeks and spending time with people who were open and honest with you. It's a bubble in time where you'll never have realer conversations with people—strangers really. There are no inhibitions about feeling a certain way and just saying it. This is in stark contrast to the rest of society, where human interaction is often kept at a superficial level of pleasantries and scripted answers to catalogued questions, a tactic I was guilty of using in an unsuccessful bid to protect myself from sharing vulnerabilities that were hard enough to manage on my own.

After going to rehab, I haven't been back. Some will make a career out of it, with addictions so serious that it's the time-out they need to keep drugs from killing them. For me, I just felt foolish. It feels odd to regret doing something that was such an expansive experience. I suppose it's guilt that prevents me from looking at it positively, guilt that I put my parents through that. I didn't have to unravel in that fashion. Sure, I could blame the writers' strike for killing my Hollywood project not more than two weeks after I drove to LA, but I should have been able to take a punch and then bounce back up, not dedicate myself to being a self-indulgent nihilist because I was pissed about the way things turned out. The real credit to my time in Tucson, though, is the supportive feeling and sense of empowerment that community can offer. I always saw myself as a solo artist, never having to lean on anyone else, never thinking others capable of understanding. Yet there, I felt at home with that immensely creative group of people—a home I'll never return to.

I ultimately realized that my problem was not with some sort of Jewish ideal that I wrestled with. I am not an archetype; I am a human being. There are all sorts of Jewish people pursuing an entire spectrum of goals and occupations. Jews are scientists, teachers, builders, doctors, bankers, athletes, computer programmers, magazine editors, etc., the same as people at large. My issue was perhaps how to fit into a capitalistic society as a creative type who doesn't do well with supervisors. How do I be someone who I am happy with? What can I do to handle disappointment better while not putting so much pressure on myself to achieve everything I want in life all at the same time? How does a young man with ADHD carve out meaning in his life and apply it to his career one day and his rebuilding process now?

Chapter 14
Post-Rehab

After landing back in New Jersey, I made my escape plans rapidly. Being in my parents' house after rehab was difficult. My level of shame about my present circumstances was never higher than when I was in constant exposure to my parents' worried stares. I knew I was basically fine and was just making it through a temporary patch of self-inflicted turbulence. Even my own perceived descent to the bottom was at least partly monitored by the levers and cranks inside my mind. Sometimes they're on overdrive and sometimes they are barely functioning; either way, it was a mechanism I felt partially in control of.

The guilt was unbearable. I had put my parents through hell. I had grossly miscalculated the effects of my actions beyond myself. I needed booze to dull the pain. I needed private space in the world where I could imbibe privately. Nobody at this stage was going to accept that I was not an addict, as a psychiatrist later confirmed. There was something else going on with me that the drinking and the drugs helped sooth, but it was not a neuro-chemical dependence. I knew this, but try telling your family your theory fresh out of six weeks in rehab. It just wasn't worth going there.

I had just enough cash from my mostly depleted 401(k) for two months' rent back in the city. It wasn't going to get me back to Manhattan, which I didn't give too much thought anyway, but Brooklyn was definitely a possibility. I found a warehouse convert in Greenpoint at the border of hipster town (Williamsburg) and a working-class Polish neighborhood in transition. The imperialistic hipsters were bleeding out in every direction in Greenpoint. The intersection of time and space I was currently occupying existed inside a window of becoming, where transitions are not quite beginning or ending. It was the perfect destination for my present state of oscillating consciousness. It made no sense, and it made perfect sense.

Of course I am in a converted warehouse in Brooklyn living with three complete strangers. Where else would I be? People with ADHD make impulsive decisions with rabid tenacity. This move was no exception. I knew I needed out and I took whatever I could find, in the fastest moment available. In the course of a month I was hired and fired as a busboy at a local restaurant and out of money completely. Credit lines were carrying me financially. I was getting obliterated by Colt 45s on a nightly basis. For the Fourth of July, I threw a party on someone else's rooftop and watched the fireworks soar with my new hipster family looking east over Manhattan, my next destination.

As summer wound down and my Hollywood dreams remained on indefinite pause, I was faced with a choice—get a job or go home. I reluctantly looked at jobs in the financial sector, given that my Series 7 was active for another five months or so. I felt like a sellout just for looking, but ideological and philosophical concerns are one thing, and being broke with no ability to pay rent is another. I had to reconcile my aversion to the white-collar world with my need to be independent. I could not go back to the magnifying glass waiting for me if I went home again, especially now that I was drinking. Its one thing for my family to say, "Yeah, he's drinking again, but he's holding down a job and paying his bills," and another for them to say, "He's drunk again, unemployed, and facedown in his mom's basement."

To me, going back to the womb was not going to be an option, so when a large and well known financial institution called me the morning after putting my résumé up online, I accepted an interview, albeit reluctantly.

* * *

I showed up to the interview in Midtown Manhattan after battling the thunderstorm that came before it. When some VP showed up to question me—a nice enough guy, I should add—and asked me for my résumé, I told him it dissolved in the rain. This was utter fantasy, and I suspect he knew it, but I suppose I said it convincingly enough that he let it slide. In banking, the ability to spit out a harmless untruth as part of a split-second reaction was a coveted and useful trait in the industry. It was at that moment, when I realized how right I was for this, that my level of self-hatred was at a blistering high. Money for freedom equated to lack of freedom for freedom. I could either go home or get a job. Both options felt like self-betrayal, though the latter came without an umbilical cord.

When I had said enough of the correct things at the interview, the VP told me when and where to go for round two. As I thanked him for his time and began to make my exit, he stopped me.

"Brian," he said. I turned around and met his gaze. "It's a sales job." I nodded in agreement. "You have to smile."

Two days later, amid an absolute downpour of sunshine, I made my way to the Upper East Side office, where I was to meet with another VP. This time I put on an immaculate Hollywood performance, for which the interviewer offered me the job flat-out after fifteen minutes of conversation. I smiled graciously, left with my paperwork, and got obliterated at the nearest Irish pub.

Psychiatrists often speak about how those with ADHD often suffer from a lesser-known phenomenon called "imposter syndrome." The idea is that in order to appear normal, someone with ADHD has to "fake it" in order to seem more engaged or blend into the situation in an acceptable manner. My sense of being an imposter during and after the interview was riding at an all-time high, and the sense was all too familiar. When you are battling the inner turmoil of your randomly generating thought process juxtaposed with the reality of social situations, the reconciliation process can be a challenge. It's not that people with ADHD are fake; that is a gross oversimplification. It's that they often struggle and don't want you to know it.

Before the interview, I had three shots of espresso, the same amount I downed before my interview with Morgan Stanley in early 2007. The best way to rev up an under-stimulated mind with the tendency to drift is to load it up with caffeine. Perhaps it's similar to the thought process behind Adderall, but without the additive, personality-altering qualities. Dr. Ned Hallowell, a noted psychiatrist specializing in ADHD and admitted ADHD sufferer, is documented as proclaiming in his book, *Driven to Distraction at Work,* that "among the medications that improve focus that are available to the general public, caffeine is by far the best." It certainly helps me process information faster and engage in conversation more steadily.

Yet, here I was—drunk again. I was alone at a bar, keeping good company with my most recent self-betrayal. *How could I take a job in finance?* I began a dialogue with myself over my third or fourth bourbon and Coke. *You left because you were outraged at yourself, abusing drugs to conceal your misery, or perhaps to cling to it harder. You ended up in the hospital and swore off the hyper-capitalistic underpinnings of a system you loathed. You are again a white young man from an upper-middle-class family who works in finance. You are inherently boring.* I waxed on and on that night about the superficialities of my worldly existence as if they were the core maxims of my interior being. I insisted on judging my own book by its cover, yet even if I was being too hard on myself, my sense of the involvement of pre-deterministic forces was palpable. I did not enjoy being broke, and couldn't cut it as a bus boy, so I had to go where I would be accepted—financial sales, of course. Shoot me in the face.

A few months later, I moved into a midtown Manhattan studio. I was still holding down the job and hating every minute of it. It was one of those big-bank atmospheres where the order and design come from high above, where the communication loses its saliency with each gradient of decadence, and where the end game is nothing more than a bunch of idiots (bankers) running around and into each other with their heads cut off and their smiles plastered in papier-mâché. The corporate hierarchy is scary, and we were the misbegotten result of an Excel spreadsheet cranked out downtown on the fifty-first floor of a corporate office made of shimmering glass and murky sunshine. We had to greet everyone the same way, take them through the same procedure. It was actually called the one-two-three drill. It was the type of soulless robotism you'd expect, and I went off script fast. I'd get yelled at for it, but not fired. When I led the branch in sales in my second month, they ignored my disregard for protocol entirely.

I may have hated the leadership, but I rather enjoyed the interaction with the bank patrons (most of them). I would drink a lot of coffee and dish out a lot of credit cards. Each credit card was worth $17.50 a pop in commission. I figured I could be doing a lot more damage in the world then extending credit, even if that credit sometimes came with high variable interest rates. I was not sex trafficking, and I was not distributing heroin in mass quantities, even if credit does have addictive properties, like morphine or Adderall. Booze was my own morphine, and the drip was constant.

I knew I was in the wrong place, yet I was back in New York, exactly where I wanted to be. I'd be at a neighborhood tavern almost nightly (until I was "eighty-sixed," which I found out means banned for life), sipping on Three Philosophers (a malty beer with a potent 9.7 percent alcohol by volume) and making friends with the other regulars. Justin Schanzer would join me occasionally, and were enjoying ourselves for the most part. Justin was a great friend and my gateway back into the Jewish community, at least in my own head. He is one of the most sincere and nicest people I have ever met. Community-conscious and cool in his own right, he would later help me get back on my feet. He had a history of showing up during some of my most unbalanced time periods, sometimes pulling me out of my own head and apartment and getting me reconnected with humanity. Simple things like football on Sundays amongst a crowd were enough to feel connected again.

I never should have ended up in rehab, I began to tell myself. I had a weak moment. I still couldn't imagine that my Hollywood dreams would not soon be realized, and that something as trivial and random as a writers' strike could take me out of the game before I ever got a chance to warm up. What did a writers' strike have to do with me? A percentage of digital royalties is no concern to a young man who is hungry just to get his work out there. It didn't matter, though. The industry was deadlocked, and there was no reason to remain in LA. Every day, every week spent in New York became too much to take. They say millennials can't take disappointment, and being born in 1983, I am on the older end of this controversial generation. To be quite honest, though, I really couldn't. The way I saw it, I had put my heart into something, taken a risk, and had fallen hard without ever even taking a step. I was meant to be successful in this endeavor. Failure was not a possibility I ever considered. And yet, I failed. Failed to begin, and failed to succeed.

Life became hollow and devoid of meaning, and so I drank. I took a flat punch to the mouth, and then numbed it with an icy bottle. Rehab taught me that drinking is not a fall-back career. I needed my job. This way I could be sober and productive until the evening, before the drip was back on line. Sure, the headaches in the morning were rough when you had to make it into work at nine in the morning, but at twenty-five years old, you can make it happen. Grab a red-eye from Starbucks and be on your way. I was getting by—"towing the line," as my dad describes it. This was not my final destination, but it would do for now.

The bar scene had a lot of upsides to it. It was like a second office. People would come meet me at the bar, or I'd drink alone; either was fine with me. Sometimes I would talk to strangers, and sometimes I would go home with one. Other times, I'd run into people I knew out of sheer coincidence.

Once particular night, I saw an old friend of mine, Heather, who had been at rehab the same time as me. We had gotten along well, and now she was back at school, attending Fordham University and studying visual arts. She was a good soul, and a creative type, rather characteristic of many of the people one meets at a detox center. She was less than detoxed, however. With a stash of cocaine in her pocket, she asked if I'd like to partake. I decided I would like to, indeed, partake. And partake we did.

It was Heather, an old high school friend of mine I was out with that night, and me, with a rolled-up ten spot and lines of white power spread out over a hardcover piece of literature. She would dump the substance from her little baggies and I'd separate them into rows with one of my credit cards. We stayed up until five in the morning doing line after line, talking about some of the most drug-fueled cosmic philosophy imaginable. She was particularly out there, going on and on about the stars and the lights. I'd say, despite the artificial mindset, we actually covered quite a lot that evening. I felt weirdly accomplished.

By the time the sky began to reveal just a hint of light, we decided to call it. My friends left, I dropped a Klonopin to slow my mind, and I went to sleep.

She was dead later that morning. Before going to sleep, she swallowed an entire bottle of her anti-anxiety meds, I later found out. She slipped into a coma and was dead by the time they found her in the early afternoon. Sweet Heather. It was devastating what she did to herself. I lamented that I had somehow contributed to her demise. I skipped work the next day tried to reconcile the foggy chain of events that led to a good girl dead at twenty years old.

The day after, I collapsed in the bathroom stall at the bank, fighting off my emotions. I knew I was not responsible for her drug use, and what I later found out to be her severe depression, but how could this happen right after my watch? How did I not see it? I had always thought that those who placed themselves in self-destructive situations, or even habitual negative behaviors, had an internal panic button as if to say, "Take a step back, abort!" I knew I had it. I enjoyed the high and the glamour that was at times emergent in risky behavior, but I was not suicidal. I was roughly in control. I thought we all were.

Heather's death was a shock to my wiring. It was absolutely harrowing, the raw reality of it. I needed to wake up. To grow up. No more mere semblance of control. I needed to be in control, so far as one can be. The randomness of the universe will exert its will on one's life path, and we can only hope to have enough internal fortitude and clarity of purpose to land somewhere in the orbit of our aspirations, in whatever form they may take. It was now time to really listen to myself, to liberate myself and seek happiness.

The manifestation of this epiphany was choppy at first.

Instead of resigning from a job I hated, I did something that I knew would get me fired. I began reversing everybody's overdraft fees who complained about them, and there were a lot of complaints on a daily basis. Indiscriminately, I must have reversed about a hundred overdraft fees back to people's checking accounts before I reversed one of my own to the tune of twenty-five dollars. There was no way I was going to get away with that. And I was right. They terminated my employment a week after meeting with an investigative compliance officer at the corporate building downtown. It wasn't much of an investigation, though. I admitted it and got out of there.

The situation was beginning to look precarious: I had no job, an apartment to pay for, and a seriously random and hazardous track record. It was mid- to late 2009 and the situation necessitated introspection so that I did not continue in a trend of self-destruction and unhappiness. I had an inkling that things could be better for me, and that I could be better to myself. I thought, *What is the one thing that forms the substrate of my philosophy and action? What is the bedrock of my defiance? What do I want in life that fuels my self-destruction, and promotes me to continuously act as the architect to my own downfall?* There must have been a pattern into which I kept sinking. *Why is the abyss unrecognizable when it's the same every time? Why am I always falling, or jumping, rather?*

I sat once again with the Three Philosophers and gave it thought. I even gave thought to the way I was thinking. Metacognition, or thinking about thinking, is helpful to find the patterns that are destructive in one's life. Thought precedes action, so if you want to understand your own actions, you need to think about the thoughts that preface them. My actions were impulsive, infused with that ADHD rapid fire that can cripple your strategic decision-making if you let it. I had been letting it, riding impulse into disaster while coming so close to fulfillment every time. Combined with the sauce, I was doing, but not being. The seedlings in my mind were spouting to action before something fully formed could root. There was no synthesis, no midway between raw idea and strategic action.

Then it hit me. Maybe it was the wisdom of the Three Philosophers, probably not my own. I had traveled back in my mind to China, where I was twenty-one and sitting at my internship with a stomachache and thinking how unlikely it was that I was going to last in a company setting. It was at that moment that I bought a domain name called Robinson Enterprises. I was dreaming of owning my own business. It wasn't the finance industry or the commonplace white-collar life that I had such acrimony toward; it was the sense that my freedom had been diminished.

Having ADHD, it is very difficult to thrive in a structured environment, hence the school and workplace troubles that are rampant among individuals with ADHD. People with ADHD are creators, but school will never train you for that. School is there to train for obedience, to be good workers. There are so many entrepreneurs who credit their success in part to their ADHD or dyslexic mind, and I have no idea why it took me so long to realize that this was my destiny as well. For those who have made the grade, and achieved success traditionally, perhaps with a graduate degree, or a VP title at a prestigious institution, I am happy for them. But that was never going to be my life, and finally I felt empowered.

Three weeks prior to this epiphany, and for the previous two and a half months before that, I had worked as a commission-only salesperson at a debt settlement firm. This was shortly after I was fired by the bank. Typically, commission-only jobs offer no security, in that you only get paid for what you bring in. Or, "you eat what you kill," as some of the more Darwinian personalities in sales atmospheres take pleasure in declaring. But as compensation for this lack of a safety net, you get a larger piece of the pie when you do bring in clients. It's a good environment for someone with ADHD, since without a salary, many of the authoritarian aspects of the corporate world are loosened up, if not completely voided. There is a lot more freedom in this type of gig. Lots of ADHD types achieve success in sales, and I was already in my comfort zone, having been a phone salesperson with Morgan Stanley years prior.

On my first day at my new gig, I had someone who was interested in their debt settlement product on the phone, and I was trying to enroll the individual. I wasn't completely sure what debt settlement was, but it was 2009 and the economy was tanking, and I had it in mind to help. Out of nowhere, while on the phone call, a middle-aged woman with oversized glasses and a voice like cigarette ash approached and told me I needed to pass the phone to her, because she was my manager. By appearance, she looked like she would be more at home serving coffee to a lethargic trucker off a major highway than telling me she was my boss. I told the person on the other end to hold and I placed him on mute. I smiled, then screamed at the manager for breaking my hyper-focus (classic ADHD trait), and insisted that nobody was my "manager." She backed off and I went back into action. After I was done with the phone call, one of the owners came up and asked me what that was all about. I replied that I wasn't here to have a manager. If I'm not on salary, and I sink or swim based on my own efforts, I'm not letting someone else step in and manage my outcome. They left me alone after that. Two weeks later, I was the manager.

I hadn't helped (the little guy, anyway) by extending so much credit in my previous job at the bank, though I don't think I can take full credit for the financial crisis or the Great Recession. You can thank the Harvard MBAs who designed those housing market derivatives for that, mainly. All I knew was that I liked the idea of settling debt rather than helping to create it. Maybe I was settling something within myself to counter-balance the self-manifested shit-storm of my last few years. I felt like I was fighting the power in my own unique way, and with this sense of purpose, I handily became this new company's number-one sales guy within the first month of my arrival.

Two months after that, I was gone. Such were the fleeting life experiences of my young life at the time. I knew I needed something more stable to commit to; I had thought I found that in Hollywood, but I was still looking. The owners ran an unorthodox work environment, and that certainly suited me, but I had issues with their product and practices, as well as a newfound mindset that set me on the verge of a decision to go out and start something myself. I wanted absolutely nobody to answer to. This is what I was seeking, and this is what I found in Churchill Credit Solutions, my own company, named after Winston Churchill, a man I admired greatly.

I spoke to some friends and family about the idea of opening my own shop and was able to raise some start-up capital, in combination with some of my own, to get operations started in my Midtown East studio apartment, the one I had recently moved into. One of my original supporters, a good friend of my parents, Ellen Cohen, who has known me since I was a small child, told me that she believes in the entrepreneur who can barely tie his own shoelaces but can run a successful enterprise. I took that as a compliment. My parents were also very supportive, expecting nothing but big things from my new venture.

My startup had a raw and tumultuous beginning. I took some of the elements of what I learned at my previous job selling debt settlement products with a few conceptual tweaks: I developed an in-house debt settlement mechanism, and I incorporated a network of attorneys to provide added consumer protection. We were helping people and small companies settle their debt. It was very difficult at first. I purchased leads from a vendor and got burned, losing a few thousand dollars in the process. The second vendor was legitimate, and I was on my way. My days consisted of speaking with complete strangers for ten hours at a time with a headset that made me feel like a jet fighter pilot, looking out to the sky as I would focus on something moving to keep my attention locked into my current verbal task.

In a year, I could accumulate a book of clients, and a new office after that. I figured out the back end, as mentioned—the debt arbitration side of it—on my own; the other company I worked for did *not* have one. Much of this involved developing a relationship with creditors and negotiating on behalf of our clients to get them out of trouble. It became perfectly exhausting as I flew through this venture in a dizzying tailspin with a focus I had never previously experienced. Hyper-focus is a blessing, but remains elusive in the mind of an ADHD individual like me. If you find yourself in this ethereal zone, figure out what got you there, and you've probably found something resembling a passion. I can't say that the subject matter of my new business was my passion, per se, but something about settling debt hit home. I felt as if I owed the universe a redemptive currency, the idea of settling, or settling up, for past indiscretions felt like a tunnel into the future, where I finally began to sense distance from an unsure state. Freedom will do that for you.

By finally listening to myself, completely, and piloting my own enterprise, I was helping others deal with their past as well. Whatever led them or their company to be in the state they were, there was no judgment, only an alternative path. Settling debt sounds boring to some, but to me, it was cathartic. It was a symbol of something great, a monument to the bold claim that anything can be turned around.

A year later, I had my own office and a handful of employees. I still went completely berserk at times, but I managed to maintain some sense of balance as my role transitioned from salesperson to manager. I felt more like an architect than a builder, though you are left with nothing but empty abstractions without both working harmoniously. Once I had the office, I was able to recruit a friend from the old debt settlement company that had ceased operations. He was able to drive sales as I developed the back end and focused on big-picture strategy. In the workplace, strategy or theorizing is ideal for the ADHD mind; execution is another story. In the beginning, I would often gloss over details even when my plan was sound. It was great to be able to consult with others over details of action. Luckily, in the real world, unlike school, there is no red pen to dock you. You can win the game in many different ways. You just need to figure out where, and within what functionality, you are most powerful. If you're not a details person, but you thrive on big-picture thinking, then pursue a creative role that demands mostly that. Don't judge yourself on the things you are not good at; team up with those who can counter-balance your strengths. The mark of school makes an imprint on the creative mindset; it leaves an impression on your self-esteem. It's hard to not be hard on yourself, something I was still struggling with at the time.

I still drank, but I kept it more functional. I would often slip out to grab a few beers at an old dive in the financial district where my office was at the time. The Irish Punt was the name of the bar, standing eternal in an increasingly yuppified neighborhood of commercial buildings and old banking high-rises converted into rentals for professionals or Manhattanites looking to get a little bit of a break on rent. A couple of beers at the old stalwart would calm my nerves and I'd be back at work.

* * *

On Wednesdays, I soon learned, there was an Irish-Swedish, silky-black-haired angel tending bar on a temporary assignment between careers. Her name was Lindsey Stokes, and I ended up marrying her.

We began to really connect on her last day on the job. She was friendly and sarcastic, and just beautiful. I felt compelled toward her in a way I've never felt for anyone or anything. Conversation synched seamlessly, action and reaction were as natural as breathing or any other involuntary, harmonic motion. I was able to get her card after expressing a light interest in her new interior design—real estate stint. I thought it would be great if she would improve the aesthetics of my Spartan chamber on the east side of Fifty-Fourth Street. I emailed her sometime later and asked her out.

Like most things in my life around that time, and certainly before, things got off to a chaotic start. I showed up drunk to our first date after lining up an early happy hour with friends, followed by a series of martinis at my grandpa's birthday dinner. By the time the hour of our date happened upon us, I was lit like *The Starry Night*, spinning in a rounded swirl of black and blue debauchery. I told her about the book I was writing about ADHD and how I needed to be more successful than my father over a succession of champagne bottles. She took it all in good stride until the end, when I was spouting utter nonsense and trying to get her to go home with me. Regrettably, I wasn't the man she deserved that night, but I took it as a challenge to be that man.

A few days later, I left her a message apologizing and asking her if she would like to do something during the day that didn't involve drinking. Miraculously, she accepted, and we went to see an Off-Broadway show. We both hated the show but loved being with each other. As weeks turned to months, we were going out steadily and exclusively. She was calm, resolute, and open-minded. She understood me to my core, yet was the opposite of me; never destructive, she possessed a fun and creative side without being impulsive or prone to sudden shifts of sanity like some of my previous girlfriends. She had the most lucid and beautiful heart of anyone I'd ever met, with an intellect of the same magnitude. She was an A student, graduating summa cum laude in college. She represented in every way the reciprocal dynamism of my being, and we fell in love. If Molly gave me the medicine I didn't need, Lindsey gave me the medicine I did need, that spiritual, through-to-the-soul type.

I'd never felt so in control as I did in my late twenties as a newly minted entrepreneur with a girlfriend I was entirely in love with. Love changes you in a lot of ways. Lindsey became a stabilizing force, especially after we moved in together and I was able to come home to her sincerity and support. I was her rock star and she my angel. While there were battles from time to time, it was mostly smooth. Occasionally, I'd be so stressed out from work, with my mind pushing its red line, and she'd tell me to get in the tub and just lay there. She'd light a candle, put on some music, and turn off the lights on her way out. Lindsey is the master of creating experiences or an environment to enhance a mood or suit a personality style. She is a true original, and a pure soul.

One day she came home and I was visibly perturbed. I told her I had just finished watching a video of a conference held by the Centre for ADHD Awareness, Canada (CADDAC), and they'd had Gina Pera as a speaker. Pera had brazenly referred to ADHD as the "elephant in the room of society." She went on about how to recognize ADHD in your partner and spoke with pleasure about how those with ADHD must be medicated. Pera is not a doctor or a therapist, yet she chooses to vigorously crusade for the medicating of individuals with ADHD as if they are all escaped mental patients on a rampage, rather than people with an alternative cognitive style.

If you try to confront Gina Pera—and I have battled her on Amazon forums multiple times—about medicating children or adults with heavy stimulants as a first and only response to ADHD, she is quick to label you "anti-science," this in a time when even the most distinguished neuroscientist will admit that we have only scratched the surface in terms of understanding how the brain works. The duality between mind and brain, or what specifically qualifies as consciousness, is hotly debated between neuroscientists, philosophers, evolutionary psychologists, etc. There is a black hole of knowledge when it comes to how the brain operates. Defining the mind, or explaining how the brain works, is right up there with attempting to define the nature of time, a concept that Einstein struggled with up until his death. Honest psychiatrists will hypothesize about how medical scientists "think" a drug works, and this has been enough to help a lot of people with a variety of mental ailments. But to dispute the efficacy of prescribing heavy stimulants to children and adult human beings for being flighty or impulsive is a whole other conversation, especially when we talk about children, who are not able to make decisions for themselves, yet have to live with the consequences.

Aside from being offensive, to categorize those with ADHD as "the elephant in the room of society" is to attempt to ostracize them or call them out as different and inferior. I told Lindsey about my concerns, and how I was roiling over this. I was taking it personally. I shouldn't have been, but I was. I saw Pera as representative of a larger force, as a minion of a propaganda machine for an industry that is worth nine billion dollars.

I was drawing radical parallels in my mind; being of Jewish descent, I saw parallels with Hitler and the Holocaust, and how it all started with isolating a group of people. It was too far, but I was going there.

Lindsey just smiled and said, "Babe, it's okay. She doesn't matter. She has no idea what she's talking about, and will never acknowledge that part of the reason you succeed is because of your ADHD. You don't need her to agree with you in order to carry on succeeding—as you. Getting in verbal sparring matches with her on ADHD Amazon forums is a waste of your time."

That's all true, and perhaps my ego *was* getting in the way. But, if ADHD is the elephant in the room of society, and I have ADHD, then I am an elephant in the room of society. That made me, and others afflicted, less than human, a nuisance. And for that I would not remain silent or passive.

In late 2016, I was interviewed on Fox 5 NY (not to be confused with Fox News) by Dana Arschin, a meticulous reporter, in a piece called "Prescription Stimulants: Controversies and Miracles." Fox was interested in presenting the story from both the vantage point of someone with ADHD and a psychiatrist who treats it. I was able to describe my frustrations growing up with ADHD, as well as my success as an entrepreneur as an adult because of it. Mathew Lorber, a psychiatrist at Lenox Hill hospital, was on record saying that children are better off on medication, while adults are probably better off not taking ADHD medicine. We are not talking about a crusading journalist here, but rather a medical doctor and psychiatrist. Lorber's position is a great middle ground that seemingly more doctors are beginning to adopt.

During a discussion with Dana about the reason Fox 5 NY showed interest in this ever-developing conflict, she made reference to a recently published *New York Times* article that covered ADHD and Adderall. The story, "Generation Adderall," was about a woman who went to Brown University and got hooked on the drug. I read it voraciously and found that her experiences were very similar to mine, including the addiction aspect. It suggested something I always suspected—there are many more out there like me. This thought brought me back to a memory of another *Times* article I read about ADHD, called "The Selling of Attention Deficit Disorder." This one was not a first-person account like the former article just mentioned, or the book I began writing in 2007. This was a chronological and historic overview of the pharmaceutical industry's tremendous growth from the distribution of ADHD drugs, and the cultural effect these drugs have on society.

Here are the facts according to this in-depth 2013 article by Alan Schwarz: 15 percent of high school children are diagnosed with ADHD and the number of children medicated for it are 3.5 million, up from six hundred thousand in 1990. "The rise of ADHD diagnoses and prescriptions for stimulants over the years coincided with a remarkably successful two-decade campaign by pharmaceutical companies to publicize the syndrome and promote the pills to doctors, educators and parents," wrote Schwarz "With the children's market booming, the industry is now employing similar marketing techniques as it focuses on adult ADHD, which could become even more profitable," Schwarz goes on to proclaim, "Sales of stimulant medication in 2012 were nearly $9 billion, more than five times the $1.7

billion a decade before."

I could go on with data and firsthand accounts about how Big Pharm marketing gets doctors to buy in with paid speaking fees and an aggressive boots-on-the-ground sales force, but that's not the point. The point is that ADHD is a big industry and a lot of people are involved for the wrong reasons. Some people on the opposite end of the spectrum will say that ADHD is completely fabricated, but a potent money-maker. I can't subscribe to that, either. ADHD is real, in the sense that there are certain traits shared among a portion of the population that manifest in similar fashions across a broad variety of people. We are spaced-out, impulsive, creative, non-conforming, dynamic, moody, hyper-obsessed, and very oppositional as children. Sometimes, one or more of these traits flares up too frequently, and with enough intensity that we get ourselves into trouble. That's the disorder part of it. You can't sugarcoat ADHD and say it's all a gift, and you can't demonize it and recommend heavy stimulants to eradicate all of the symptoms. The balance, and the truth, is that ADHD is both a gift and a disorder. If you think it's only one or the other, you are missing the big picture.

* * *

John Locke was a famous seventeenth-century British philosopher who wrote extensively on the theory of knowledge. To summarize, his theory revolves around the "tabula rasa," or blank slate, and the assertion that knowledge is obtained as we build upon this blank slate like the construction of a building, the framework for which is obtained through ideas laid down as concepts. In other words, the purpose of knowledge is to build an intricate framework of concepts that can mold together and universally connect as we as humans come into contact with more and more seemingly isolated ideas. We are constantly building upon what we already know in order to gain a more complex, holistic body of knowledge and understanding of the world we live in. Somewhere along the line, the educational system lost track of this understanding, and instead of instilling in its students a global perspective of knowledge and thought, it began instead to compartmentalize facts and ideas so that they remain merely isolated colonies of thought without any sort of unifying framework.

Perhaps the reason for this is that society is more concerned with training our minds to think in parts of a whole because one day, for the sake of the economy, we will have to choose a specialization of some sort for our occupations. Our minds are becoming more suited for the tiny little cubes most workers will call their desks, representing a small part of a rather large institutional whole, like isolated atoms of thought orbiting with a loose connectivity to the larger molecule, easily swayed by the next attractive charge, and ultimately lost in a web of disassociation. For the sake of the economy, I do not have a problem with an educational system that wishes to ensure the livelihood of tomorrow, but we are needlessly suppressing the type of thinking that will ultimately lead to innovation for the sake of being well schooled in the types of things we have already figured out. There are leaders and there are followers, and in many cases, one must be a follower in order to become a leader, but if we continue to educate students like sheep in a herd through repetition of solutions to problems already solved, then we will only be a nation representative of an antiquated solution to an antiquated problem.

If, on the other hand, we can encourage the type of creative thinking not tied down to any problem in particular, but rather representative of the type of thought process involved in universal concepts and creative solutions, we can rid ourselves of the shackles of intellectual underachievement as a society and branch out toward a renewed global presence and respect among the powerhouses of the East. I am not saying that we should by any means stop teaching the same solutions to the same problems entirely, as these solutions represent the bedrock of intellectual and academic advancement in history. What I am saying is we ought to focus more on the thought process behind the intellectuals who lead us to these solutions in the first place to gain a better understanding of where true academic leadership derives itself.

When there is the assumption that everyone is inside the box and thinking outside of it is like taking a break from a regularly scheduled activity, you teach to the exclusion of those who live their life OUTSIDE THE BOX. For me, thinking inside the box is sometimes just as hard as it is for someone else to think outside of it. For one, I have trouble thinking about one specific idea without attempting to generalize and connect this idea as a concept with a seemingly altogether different domain of knowledge.

Sometimes, amid my attempt to make connections, I will stumble upon altogether different ideas, far away from where I started, though still relevant in its own way.

Chapter 15
ADULT ADHD

Society is finally at the point where its members don't have to answer to anybody they don't choose to. Technology now outpaces the speed of the human mind. The adaptive traits of ADHD are never more useful as today. The techno-culture has created a world where the ADHD mind is right at home.

As an adult, I've found that I can understand my mind in a way I just couldn't as a kid. I know my thinking is overwhelmingly visual, and it feels like having multiple windows open at once, each containing a different task or concept. I can have a window open—or half of a screen, like on a computer—while working simultaneously on something else, also half of a screen. This is a horrible thing to deal with in school, where your attention must be on one thing at a time, often to memorize for regurgitation later. And yet it is a wonderful thing to deal with as an entrepreneur.

If I'm dealing with three people in my company speaking to me at the same time, all while crunching numbers on my calculator, the ability to broaden my net of attention is useful. It's similar to the way a multi-core microprocessor can handle several different "threads" at once. We are living in a world where information is coming simultaneously in short spurts from numerous sources all day. Between our smart phones, people in the real world, and our email on our various screens, our collective consciousness officially has ADHD now. Society is more hyper than ever. So, do you want to take Adderall to focus on one thing, or do you want to embrace the chaos of it all?

I haven't taken Adderall since 2007, the year I ended up in the hospital after hallucinating about being Jesus. Those days are gone. I'm no longer trying to pass a test after test after test. It's easy to think that grades are what make you successful later in life, especially when you belong to a culture that demands academic achievement from its children. Please understand: Grades can be important for certain career tracks, but they are not the only measure of intelligence, and they certainly don't weigh heavily on the success of creative people. ADHD is a creative mindset, among other things. You can't listen very well in school, you can't sit still for very long without putting something in motion (typically your legs), and you're not very good at following directions, especially in a subject that bores you. But you are brilliant in so many other ways.

When I was a kid, I used to read a lot. Reading is something you can do on your own terms; you can pick the subject matter and follow your own path to knowledge. I did that in college, often focusing more on books I chose than those assigned by my curriculum. It's just the way I was wired. Then, suddenly, I wasn't in school anymore. I got my bachelor's, which is bare minimum for a Jewish gentleman like myself, and I was done. I was lucky enough to go to college, and I passed. It was a tremendous experience, and I do think people should be forced to learn boring subjects to help create a bedrock of conceptual structure. But a person with ADHD is likely not going to do as well as others in the prevailing system of education, and the more we can de-emphasize grades and emphasize pursuing passion, the better off alternative learners will be.

The real world is something else. It's the big show. If you have drive, you can do anything. All of the sudden, doing what you want to be doing is not happening at the cost of what you ought to be doing. Doing what you want to be doing can be the main event. It took me a bit of time to realize this. At Morgan Stanley, I still had the mentality that my ultimate success would come after passing as many tests as possible. Instead of enjoying the ride and picking up knowledge at a healthy pace, I was maniacal about achieving. Adderall was the anti-ADHD drug, and ADHD was what was holding me back from reaching my potential. I needed more Adderall than prescribed because it was never going to be enough to make up for a young life history of underachievement.

The Adderall kicked me on the floor while I was bleeding. I was kicking myself. I ended up in California, arrogant and on a mission to rectify everything. I was on the floor again. This sick obsession with succeeding, as if I could even define it at the time, drove me repeatedly into anger and depression. I was somehow caged by my own expectation of myself, which I thought were prescribed to me from the outside world, but really it was in my head the entire time. For a long time, I couldn't recognize it, or even if I did, I knew of no way to get out. And yet, looking back, it was all about freedom; being free and charging up with my own ideas. It was a fine time in my life when I realized that I will not and cannot ever work for anyone else again. As an adult, I will ride high or sink on my own terms.

* * *

These days, I'm good. I have support, and people around me who understand me. I don't drink more than a couple times a week, and it's under control. Not everyone with a past substance abuse problem is an addict, as I was able to prove to myself. Since age twenty-seven when I started my business, I have been focused. It's tough sometimes when you take something on that is supposed to eventually work out, but if you come in every day and put forth the effort, it will pay off. This is hard to accept; the ADHD mind craves instant gratification. I was working from 10 a.m. to 9 p.m. for years trying to fast-track progress, but there is only so much that can be humanly done. Critical mass requires massive amounts of energy over a long period of time. The key is to keep showing up every day.

It's hard to fathom why anyone would want to put themselves in a position where nothing is guaranteed in return for the work you put in. For those who work hard, collect a salary and go home, trust me, I get it. Getting paid for your work is something ingrained in a person since they were a kid and their parents would give them an allowance. Take the trash out, get paid. Study hard, get an A on the test. This is how we are bred, so to voluntarily put yourself in a position where there is no security, no clear line to success, must be insane. But that's what I loved about it. Starting out with a blank slate is completely exhilarating. I remember wanting to paint this open space with furious brush strokes, bringing it into being from the infant concept to the actualization of an enterprise in a rush.

Lindsey was especially supportive while I was building, continuing to throw me in the bathtub and light more candles to help calm my nerves. Being an entrepreneur is not glamorous. Often, you feel like you are at war. And you are. Every day my emotions would bend like hot steel into something I couldn't return from. The ADHD hyper-focus is not always a good thing, as it makes it very difficult to switch gears sometimes. It's not easy to leave work at work when everything is swirling in your brain all at once. I couldn't always defocus to refocus. Early in our relationship, Lindsey would call me and I would be at a bar getting lit in the financial district. My employees didn't always need supervision, I justified. It wasn't all the time, but it was frequent enough that it put stress on our relationship. Thankfully, as I eclipsed thirty, I learned to cope better with stress and redirect in any flooding emotions into a healthier drainage outlet.

Growth was key. Growth of the company and my own growth spiritually and emotionally. I still struggle, at times, to keep my temper in check, but five years with an angel of a woman will optimize the person you become. I owe Lindsey everything for her patience and willingness to explore and understand the ways of my being. I sometimes think she took on more than she bargained for, but most times I rationalize that she took on exactly what she bargained for. Somehow, there exists a woman who is wholly for me, and I for her. She was always going to marry an entrepreneur type, but some people say that without knowing what kind of person thrives in that sort of light. She always knew, partly because in that respect, we are the same.

She could have married someone with a more stable paycheck (or mind, for that matter), but she chose someone who was building something. Her father is a builder; literally, he builds with his bare hands, using hammers, nails, wrenches, anything. The man built a fireplace from floor to ceiling using massive stones he found in nature, while his young daughter at the time, Lindsey, assisted with the smaller acquisitions. I always joke that it's a tough act to follow, being a Jewish guy married to the daughter of a builder, when something breaks in the apartment or is in need of repair. Her father would just build a new one, whatever it was: a wall, a rocking chair, an entire house. I have to call Geek Squad just to mount a TV. Somehow, we make it work.

Lindsey and I once built the Eiffel Tower out of Legos. It was a three-hundred-plus-piece set that we worked on painstakingly until the final spire was placed gently on top. It took me back about a year prior, when we were on the real Eiffel Tower in Paris for our second anniversary.

I was looking out into the distance, poring over the infinite cityscape, and I said over the wind, to Lindsey, "You know, I'm feeling something I can't put my finger on. It's like an emotion I'm not quite used to, or haven't felt in a long time."

She turned and spoke after a brief moment of consideration. "It's happiness. You're happy, babe."

And so I was. The past was settled and the future seemed glorious even then; it especially does now, so long as I am with her, and the baby developing inside of her.

Chapter 16
Mental Nationalism

Things are looking good for me and my expanding family, and our future looks bright. I have resolved most of the issues that were bothering me from the past and writing this manuscript has proved to be quite cathartic. I feel blessed that I can finally express myself through this medium, as there has been so much building up inside me for so long. I fret that without such an outlet, the pressure inside would burst in a less productive and far more destructive manner, as it has too many times in the past. My ego was shot for a long time after high school; I experienced significant social and emotional withdrawal, a very unhealthy duo of complicated human responses. Looking back, as sequentially as I can manage, I believe I have found the roots of most my problems, though to have come this far, there is one thing I am fortunate to know I will never lose, as it has already been put to the test, and that is my undying faith in myself. Through it all, I never stopped believing in myself; I have always been meant for more, despite what it seemed at certain times for me.

I have lost a lot of friends throughout my journey, before my renewal in California, where I began to make many new ones. If my older friends are reading this now, I am sorry. I never meant to hurt anyone, though I acknowledge that I was not a good friend to certain individuals during my years of withdrawal, and

I am regretful. I spent a lot of time with myself, alone, trying to figure out a way to translate the complexity of the thoughts in my mind in a way that would be productive for me. For a couple years, starting midway through college, I was truly lost. I was always searching for something else, as nothing made sense for a long time. Luckily, I have found what I was looking for, and I am marching to the tune of redemption, not only for myself but for others like me. As a kid, I was trapped; as a teenager, I was numb; and as a college student, I was destructively curious and reflective. Now, as a young adult, I would like to think of myself as wise. I have seen and felt a lot, and at the risk of a cliché, I truly believe with all my heart that one person really can make a difference, and that we all deserve that chance.

With my chance, I want to call for freedom. Not to be confused with anarchy, but rather a matter of liberation, so to speak. I am calling for liberation from psychiatric diagnoses that do more harm than good. I am especially calling for the immediate halt in the over-prescribing of dangerous personality-altering, soul-diluting drugs. What people need to realize is that there is no absolute truth, only schools of thought, and when the masses of society lean in one direction, so too does their frame of mind. They may not realize that they are blindly accepting a system of thought that is not necessarily correct, but merely agreed upon by enough people that it is accepted as truth. I want to put a stop to all of this.

One thing has changed in my thinking since I first started this book: It's not the schools' fault. I began this book speaking about how underappreciated minds are falling through the cracks of the educational system, that would-be scientific innovators, entrepreneurs, and creative thinkers in general are getting an early start with low self-esteem. However, many schools are doing the best they can by teaching in the manner in which the majority learns well. The creative ADHD types are unique, in that school will never be the place where they validate themselves, or their intelligence. Now that I am going to have my own kid, if she has ADHD, I will tell her not to put too much pressure on grades, to extract knowledge from lessons for the sake of knowledge, not for a test. I might get that opportunity soon. I think we can improve the self-esteem of kids with ADHD or alternative learners by letting them know that the school system was not built for their exact likeness, and that neither is life. What these kids need to know is that they are exceptional anyway, and that they need to find their talents outside of the structure, and once they do, they need to pursue it with everything they have.

I want the school system to wake up, however, and realize that there is a new breed of children emerging in epic proportions. They are out-of-the-box thinkers, many with learning challenges, many of them gifted. Whatever it is, when there is oppression of the few, for the sake of the betterment of the many, expect a thunderous rebellion from those strong enough to recognize and act upon the need for change. It's a movement I call "mental nationalism." Here is what it means: Just as countries and states have borders—nationalistic borders, that is—so too does the individual. Liberate your mind from antiquated systems of thought and will your own meaning upon the world, and do it with passion. A free thinker wages war on oppressive systems and threats just as a state or country would. If you don't harm me, I won't harm you. I say live and let live, but if you start telling me how to think, or come at me violently, I will give it back to you threefold. This is what I call progress.

* * *

I am now liberated and refuse to be depressed, having lived a life by the dictates of Judaism. If I don't want to recite Hebrew, then I won't. If I choose to give the idea of God more thought as I grow and live through new experiences, rather than having the idea shoved down my throat like when I was young, I will. If you choose to debate with me, have at it. If a rabbi comes to my house and tries to guilt-trip me into "honoring" him by attending one of his services, I will tell him no, I don't mean any disrespect, but I cannot do that. I am free to decide, and so, too, is the rest of this world.

If I am in school and the teacher is trying to indoctrinate me with an idea or thought that I am opposed to, then I am going to state my rebuttal, and they have every right to state their own, and we can go back and forth until one of us is right or we agree to disagree. But as far as authority is concerned, we need to realize that it is a very relative concept, and in reality, authority is only as potent and real as we actively subject ourselves to it. This is something that I realized at a very early age.

If someone calls you ADD, perhaps someone with "authority" representing a pseudo-science such as psychology or psychiatry, you have every right to say, "Okay, maybe this is a positive thing, and this person can help me out with life and the tribulations surrounding it." But if you care to rise above society's labels and declare yourself to be simply an individual, you have every right to do so. *Do* I have ADHD? Well, that's what a doctor said a long time ago. Stupid, meaningless labels. The truth is that I am what I am—a unique individual.

I challenge every parent who reads this today, who is dealing with a younger version of a kid similar to me, to take a good look at exactly what you are dealing with. If he or she is sitting in a classroom, daydreaming or disrupting because their mind is not wired like the rest of the class, the last thing you should do is force them to conform. I'd say, if anything, do your best to create an environment that better suits a soaring imagination. Discover the reason for their lack of attention toward what the other children are sitting nicely at their desks for. If you work with your kid, they will work with you, if not, these independent minds will find a way to express themselves in a very different, and much more destructive manner.

I will end where I began: an individual's ability—or disability—is relative to mental environmental factors. I used to hurl bricks through the windows of unfinished construction sites to release anger. In college, I boozed and did drugs while purposefully choosing to read books outside of the curriculum. Sure, it didn't help my GPA, but there was no question I was getting smart. Perhaps I was rebelling; more than likely I was just following my interests. I read *Mein Kampf*, an autobiographical book by Adolf Hitler, just to get inside the head of my enemy. I wondered how a struggling artist like the goofy-looking bastard named Adolf could possibly transform a nation into a political tyranny through the illogical rants in his book and his speeches. There is really only one answer: Because people let him.

We need to abolish notions of categorization. I am an apolitical person calling for mental nationalism. Live and let live; protect your mental borders; and be careful when crossing the mental borders of others, especially mine if you mean to inflict your belief system on my domain.

If I'm thinking in pictures about Jupiter's gravitational orbit around the Sun, and you are trying to tell me how great it was that Abraham was going to slay his son Isaac on top of a mountain, then we are not communicating, and I am going to let you know. With proper communication, we can have peace, from student to teacher, from blue state to red state, from the first world to the third world, and back around again to the fundamental atoms of thought that represent the fabric of my consciousness.

CPSIA information can be obtained
at www.ICGtesting.com
Printed in the USA
LVHW031950261119
638523LV00002B/258/P